INGREDIENTS
—— OF ——
OUTLIERS

A RECIPE FOR PERSONAL ACHIEVEMENT

JOHN SHUFELDT, MD, JD, MBA

Inquiries should be addressed to:
Outliers Publishing
7332 E. Butherus Drive
Scottsdale, AZ 85260

ISBN: 978-1-940288-00-0

Printed in the United States of America

Cover design by Fabrizio Romano of The Forza Design

Interior design and layout by Perfect Bound Marketing + Press

Manuscript review by Bob Kelly of WordCrafters, Inc.

Author photograph by Kat C. Smith

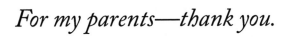

For my parents—thank you.

TABLE OF CONTENTS

INTRODUCTION

Outlier: an exceptional person for whom excellence is merely a starting point toward a destination far beyond our normal definition of achievement.

I was standing in front of a group of individuals, all belonging to MENSA (The International High IQ Society), having just given a talk on self-leadership and entrepreneurism, and I thought it went fairly well. God knows, I'd never qualify for MENSA, so the fact that I was invited to speak to this distinguished group left me a bit perplexed.

Nevertheless, after the discussion, I was asked a number of questions. One of them, which I'll never forget, left me speechless. "This is all well and good," said a gentleman from the back of the room, "and we're all very excited to go out and accomplish things. But tomorrow morning when we wake up and look in the mirror, it won't be John Shufeldt. It will just be *us* standing there, and we'll be the same person we were the before your talk, and nothing will have changed. What do you have to say to that?"

Not only did his statement seem to suck every bit of air out of the room, it also got me thinking. If this high IQ group felt they were struggling to make a difference, how could the rest of us possibly survive, let alone compete?

What makes someone a standout—an outlier? What ingredients make outliers unique, and where can the rest of us find those ingredients? Thus began my search to find that "secret sauce," those special ingredients in the recipe which when combined make an individual an outlier.

I'm getting a bit old—at least that's what my kids tell me. Along my journey, I've had some fantastic experiences and met some amazing people who taught me, again and again, that we all have the necessary ingredients to become an outlier. We just need to remember them.

The people I've met or cared for as a physician have come from all walks of life, from different ethnicities, and from varied educational and religious backgrounds. Some have taught me how to conduct myself. Others have taught me exactly how to *not* conduct myself. I've learned something from each of them and appreciate all the lessons.

I was adopted from an orphanage before my memory took hold. My parents were hard working, loving, strict, and honest. They gave me every opportunity imaginable and supported my older sister and me as best as they knew how.

The one thing I lacked, and would change if I could, is that I wasn't fortunate enough to be introduced to a mentor—someone who would have opened doors, kicked me in the rear end, or patted me on the back, as necessary. In the Navy, this role is called a Sea Daddy—someone who takes a less-experienced crewmember under his or her wing and expert tutelage.

I take complete responsibility for my lack of a mentor; I simply did not put myself out there to investigate the possibilities of what a mentor could do to help me. Consequently, I was my own best and worst counsel and, subsequently, I made lots of mistakes along the way. Persevering through these mistakes, and reading books, as well as watching others, became my pseudo-mentor.

The genesis of this book is simply to remind myself, and tell others, what insights a mentor would have shared with me if he or she had the chance. These chapters are by no means industry specific, nor are they all-inclusive. The stories shared and the insights gained apply to all endeavors — personal and professional.

Not all of them will apply to you. Most of them you already know and may just need a simple reminder. Over the years, I've found that most everyone I've shared these ideas with has substantial experience and more than a passing understanding of the concepts. However, because learning is lifelong and memory is sometimes short, the following pages are not only reminders to me, but to you.

The term "outliers" came into the forefront of my vocabulary after reading Malcolm Gladwell's book: *Outliers: The Story of Success*. In it, he argues that success in any field requires practicing a specific task for at least 10,000 hours. He also discusses the different variables which contribute to a person achieving extreme success. In an article in *USA Today*, Gladwell was quoted as saying, "The biggest misconception about success is that we do it solely on our smarts, ambition, hustle and hard work." I agree. Success—at least in the business, sports, and entertainment worlds—takes a myriad of activities, a measure of luck, and some God-given talent.

I'm not simply talking about the tangibles (I.Q., strength, speed, agility) and intangibles (birth order, where you were born, and what your parents taught you) that go into making someone successful. Although some measure of "success" will come from following the ideas shared in this book, demonstrable success measures only a fraction of the capacity each of us has to "alter our own stars" and rescript our own future.

My goal in writing this book is to remind the readers that outliers walk among us, and that anyone can become "markedly different in value [and value(s)] from the rest of the sample." In others words, you too can be less worried, more productive, more positive, and more secure. It's actually very easy—turn the page, and let's get on with it.

Humility: The Root of Success

No man thinks there is much ado about nothing
when the ado is about himself.
~ Anthony Trollope

The ego! We all have one, and it's neither good nor bad. It simply means "self." The problem begins when it becomes a dominant, pervasive, and consuming factor in our lives. In the extreme it's called egotism or egocentricity, defined as "the practice of talking about oneself too much," or "an exaggerated sense of self-importance." The late, great football coach Frank Leahy, of Notre Dame fame, aptly described egotism as "the anesthetic which dulls the pain of stupidity."

Of course, it was hard for me to develop "an exaggerated sense of self-importance" when the needle on my talent-meter was appropriately pointing squarely at mediocre—or worse! Growing up in the 60s and 70s, I played nearly every sport available to kids. You name it—football, basketball, boxing, baseball, etc. I was mediocre at them all. I was slow, I couldn't jump, and I didn't have a head for the ball.

To make matters worse, I didn't have much of a killer instinct, so my father used to smack me on the side of the head before boxing matches.

He told me he was attempting to get me mad at my next opponent. I remember very clearly telling him I was getting a headache and only getting mad at *him*. Or, to quote the kid who was getting shocked by Dr. Venkman (Bill Murray) in *Ghostbusters*: "I can tell you what the effect is, it's *pissing me off!*"

Most of my athletic career was spent on various benches, collecting a variety of wooden splinters and only getting to play long after the outcome was decided. It wasn't that I didn't care. I really cared. It was simply that other than being tall, I possessed a paucity of God-given physical talent.

To overcome some of my athletic shortcomings, I practiced like I was possessed. I spent an entire year shooting a thousand shots a day at the basketball hoop on my driveway. I even shoveled the driveway in the winter so I could shoot. Nonetheless, in high school I was cut from the sophomore basketball team, even after making two free throws in a row, which was the *quid pro quo* for making the team.

I finally managed to make the team for my junior and senior years, but spent the majority of the time on the bench. I was just slightly better in track and field. During my freshman year in high school, I joined the track team as a pole vaulter. When the high jumper out-jumped me, despite the long pole I was carrying, I switched to discus. By the time I was a senior, I was one of the better discus throwers in our district. Don't be impressed; it's like saying I was the tallest midget. Anyway, with the discus, I actually achieved some measure of success.

I was a walk-on to the track team at Drake University. My discus career in college was cut short after I released the discus early and accidentally threw it into a crowd of runners during the 10,000-meter race at the Arkansas Relays. Regrettably, the most notable thing I accomplished in my track "career" was almost maiming a few of the Somali runners and nearly inciting an international incident just short of Mogadishu. Black Hawk Down would have had nothing on me.

While I was quite bad at sports, I was worse in school. I used to pretend I was asleep when my parents returned from parent-teacher conferences. I suspect they had some indication of my grades because I'd be heading off to bed at 6 p.m. Although I really tried at sports, I didn't exert much effort in school. My high school grades were rarely higher than a very occasional B. I believe I received more Ds than Bs. Ultimately, I graduated in the bottom quartile of my high school class.

Given my past experiences and lack of success, the burden of a large ego is not something I've had to endure.

The Gear Horn

There's an old saying that goes, "There's no such thing as a complete failure; you can always be used as a bad example." One guy who more than met that definition was a pilot named Bobby who had a hangar next to mine at Falcon Field (Arizona) Airport. Bobby had a massive ego regarding his flying skills, despite more than one case of failing to lower his landing gear, resulting in what is known as a "gear-up" landing. Such landings, of course, cause significant damage to the plane and runway and certainly don't enhance the pilot's reputation for safety.

After the first crash, the FAA held an inquiry and Bobby reportedly blamed his copilot for the failure to lower the landing gear. He got off almost scot-free, save for the wrecked aircraft and momentarily damaged (yet still monumental) ego. Not long afterward, Bobby experienced his second gear-up landing, this time while piloting a rare, old, and irreplaceable military plane. He reportedly said, "At least I stayed on the centerline!" That's akin to sailing the Titanic into the iceberg and saying, "Hey, at least I missed the penguin!"

Gear-up landings are remarkable for many reasons. When a plane's airspeed drops below a certain point, the gear warning horn automatically starts going off. It's so obnoxious and loud that it's impossible to mistake it for anything else, and should cause the pilot to lower the gear, if for no other reason than to stop the unbearable noise.

Unfortunately, there are lots of folks like Bobby out there, in every field of endeavor you can name. Their egos are so bloated that they don't hear the "gear warnings" going off. They'll do things their way, with little or no regard for common sense, sound judgment, and established procedures.

Over the years, I've seen many other examples of egotism in action and the outcomes are invariably bad. To make matters worse, the egotist will not only fail to take responsibility for these negative outcomes but, like Bobby, will often blame others for what happened. In the business world, being on the receiving end of this can be financially painful.

I recently lived through one of these episodes. I was in an urgent care start-up with a couple of individuals who had absolutely no idea about how to manage a medical practice. It wasn't that they weren't competent; they simply had no experience. For most of us, the lack of experience would cause us to "go long" on listening and absorbing, and "short" on speaking and acting. However, these two had the behavior reversed, to the detriment of themselves and others. Contrast that to the medical world—where arrogance can cost a life.

It happened like this. A nurse came to one of our emergency room attending physicians, concerned about the condition of a very ill child, to which the physician responded, "When you get your medical degree, come back and we'll chat about it." The physician, believing his authority or competence was being threatened, followed up with, "Now, discharge the patient." The nurse obliged and the child had a bad outcome. Sadly, it happens again and again.

A Botched Surgery—and Borderline Personality

During my third year of medical school, an extremely unpleasant encounter with a couple of egotistical cardiothoracic (heart) surgeons caused me to change my lifelong career plans. Had I not met these two instrument-throwing, ass-grabbing madmen, I might have become a heart surgeon. Frankly, they scared me to death. It wasn't only their complete lack of regard for human life; it was their utterly narcissistic behavior.

During a difficult surgery to repair a mitral valve in the heart of an elderly woman, my job was to hold her heart up to improve the exposure while she was on bypass. The surgeons initially sized the prosthetic valve incorrectly and had to remove it and re-sew a smaller artificial valve in the heart. Unfortunately, by this point she'd been on the pump for about 90 minutes and the tissue surrounding her mitral valve was so fragile that they were never able to adequately sew the new valve into place.

All the while, I stood rock-still holding her non-beating heart, breathing shallowly so as not to move even a fraction of an inch while they were attempting to re-stitch the valve into place. Ultimately, the poor woman never came off the bypass pump, and she died in the operating room.

These two surgeons became unhinged—throwing instruments, blaming everyone in sight except themselves. Their egos refused to let them accept any responsibility for this woman's death. This one incident scarred me for life.

Changing Course

Until that very moment, for as long as I could remember, I had wanted to be a heart surgeon. Never mind that I barely made it out of high school. I'd been reading books about famous and pioneering cardiac surgeons, such as Michael DeBakey and Denton Cooley, since I was a kid.

I remember leaving the operating room thinking no one could be this malignant and get into medical school. It must have been their training, which contributed to, or even caused, the deterioration into their pro-fanity-laced temper tantrums. In many respects, it was a by-product of their misplaced egotism that I ended up in emergency medicine.

I suppose lessons, good and bad, are unveiled daily. You just have to be open-minded enough to listen. In retrospect, very few physicians are that arrogant and, as I learned later, their training had little to do with their behavior. I'm sure they'd been complete jerks for the better part of their adult lives. Nevertheless, it so unnerved me that I changed my direction and found my home in emergency medicine which, given my short attention span, proved to be a much better choice.

Easy Prey

A physician friend told me a story about Bellevue Hospital in New York City. It happened very early one morning. Until about 2 a.m., the emergency department "ED" was getting crushed with patients suffering from various problems such as overdoses, gunshot wounds, and everything in between.

There was a lull in the onslaught, and for the first time the ED physicians—covered with blood, vomit, and grime—were finally able to sit down for a moment's rest. Just as they did, the pneumatic doors opened and a man staggered in. One of the residents said, "Oh Lord, help me… not another drunk!" Just then, the man fell flat on his face with an arrow sticking out of his back. The other resident stood up and yelled, "Circle the wagons!"

People with large egos are much like the poor guy shish kebabbed by the arrow. They have a large target on their backs. It's easy to take advantage of someone whose ego prevents him or her from seeking assistance. For example, physicians are often seen as making poor business decisions. I suspect the root cause is that many of us think, "How hard can this be? I made it through medical school."

In reality, many aspects of business, law, and medicine are very challenging and people can get in over their heads quickly in areas where they lack the background, the training, or the experience. Unscrupulous individuals know how to play right into this weakness.

It goes something like this:

> **Salesperson:** "Doctor, what's your opinion about investing in real estate?"

Doctor: "For my money, I think the stock market may offer a better hedge against our current market."

Salesperson: "Interesting. So what you're saying is that using derivatives as a hedge against market volatility is where you want to put your money. I hadn't considered that as an option."

Doctor (not knowing the first thing about derivatives): "Right, hedging in this market is smart."

Salesperson: "I hadn't thought about it until you mentioned it, but I have an opportunity for you that does exactly what you're advising..."

You can see where this is going. Ask a person with a huge ego enough questions and you'll get him to say something close to where you want him to end up. Paraphrase it back in the exact form you want it. Tell him how brilliant he is for coming up with it and you have him! Sounds completely transparent? Absolutely, and it happens every day.

The Flip Side

Do these stories suggest that egotism is an unavoidable occupational hazard for doctors as well as for other successful professionals and business leaders? Absolutely not. For every egotist I've met, I've known many men and women who consistently display the opposite character trait—humility.

It was the late author Frederick L. Collins who captured both the egotistical and the humble in these words: "Always remember there are two types of people in the world: those who come into a room and say, 'Well, here I am!' and those who come in and say, 'Ah, there you are.'" The choice is ours.

I once heard humility described as "a strange thing. The moment you think you've got it, you've lost it." The late author Helen Nielsen compared it to underwear: "essential, but indecent if it shows."

The Burger Salesman

Recently a colleague of mine, a former bank president, told me of a lesson he'd unexpectedly learned many years ago. A stranger came into the bank lobby and approached one of the officers about cashing a check. He presented identification and while his check was being approved and processed, the officer, simply passing time, asked him what he did for a living.

The man said simply, "I sell hamburgers." After receiving his cash, he expressed his thanks and left.

When the president asked the officer the stranger's name, he showed him the check. The name on it, which the young officer hadn't recognized, was Ray Kroc. Twenty years earlier, the then 55-year-old Kroc had launched what would become a nationwide—and later worldwide—chain of hamburger restaurants: McDonald's. By the time of that bank visit, Kroc was famous and his company had sold hundreds of millions of hamburgers.

Kroc saw no need to inform that banker of his business empire or mention his achievements. His simple answer to that question was characteristic of his humility. For example, whenever he was acclaimed as an overnight success, he'd simply reply: "I was an overnight success all right, but 30 years is a long, long night."

Over the years, I've been fortunate to be involved in a lot of amazing things and to meet some phenomenally gifted people. For example, and in no particular order, they've included state and United States Supreme Court justices, surgeons and physicians at the top of their game, philanthropists, billionaires, SEAL team members, fighter pilots, politicians, writers, speakers, rock stars, test pilots—the list goes on and on.

The one trait common to all of the "real deals" has been a profound humility. Like Ray Kroc, they didn't brag or overwhelm the conversation; they haven't gone on and on telling me about themselves or name dropping. They haven't needed to—they're simply and quietly confident. I'd like you to meet some of them.

Somebody's Mom

I serve on the Board of Trustees for Drake University where I graduated in 1982 with degrees in criminology and sociology. Drake wasn't always the highly regarded academic institution it is today. I was told when I applied that it was called the "Harvard of the Midwest."

Full disclosure: the year I was accepted (1978), Drake took in more than 90 percent of the applicants, the highest acceptance rate in its history. On seeing my high school grades, whoever was calling Drake the "Harvard of the Midwest" should have been dismayed. In fact, if I applied today, or during any other period of the school's history, I'd never get in.

As board members, we meet on a quarterly basis, acting as stewards and fiduciaries of the institution. I enjoy it immensely. What I enjoy most is meeting with students. They're smart, motivated, articulate, and still have that "shiny new car" sheen. Board members often meet for lunch with various student groups and sit among the students who are, as a rule, not shy about sharing their thoughts about the university —or, for that matter, anything!

At one of these lunches, I was paired with a new board member and about five students. The areas the students were exploring and writing research papers about were unbelievable—cutting-edge ideas just over the horizon. I learned a ton from them.

As this was all about the students, I shared little about myself, and the new board member I was seated next to shared nothing about her background. She asked a few questions but otherwise sat listening intently to the students with a warm smile on her face. In fact, I only knew her first name, Marsha. If I had to describe her it would be, "She's somebody's mom." I'm not even sure what I mean by that. She simply looked warm, engaging, nonjudgmental, and friendly—someone's mom.

After lunch, we walked back to the meeting and I had the chance to do a bit of cyber-stalking on my phone. I looked at the board website and figured out her last name was Ternus. I still had no idea who she was until I googled her name. Marsha Ternus was the former Chief Justice of the Iowa Supreme Court. In fact, she was the first female Chief Justice in the history of that court.

Little did I know, Marsha Ternus is a "rock star." Her presence on the Drake board will be positively felt by the entire university for years to come. Yet, there she was quietly sitting among a group of students who were excitedly discussing their research, while she selflessly and humbly listened to their sometimes overly detailed (and often over my head) explanations.

Follow Me Out!

Terri is a vivacious marketing and public relations expert we employed at *NextCare*. She and her sister Tracy are twins and give new meaning to the word "identical." They finish each other's sentences, laugh before the punch lines of each other's jokes, and enjoy a sameness shared only by twins. Remarkably, they each married fighter pilots.

Terri is married to Aaron, an F-16 (Viper) pilot, whose last deployment was flying lead solo with the Air Force Thunderbirds. Aaron was simply the best of the best. He looked, acted, and was every bit a walking recruitment poster for Air Force aviation. One of Aaron's most endearing qualities is humility. Despite his accomplishments, his war record, and his rapid rise through the ranks of the Air Force, Aaron is as low key and as humble as anyone you'll ever meet. Although he has "rock star" status, this vignette is not about him.

It was through Aaron and Terri that I met Tracy's husband Matt. Matt is an Air Force Academy graduate who was also a Viper pilot. He was one of a select group of pilots chosen to first fly the F-35. Officially named the Lockheed Martin F-35 Lightning II, this single-seat, single-engine fifth-generation fighter aircraft was designed for multiple roles, including ground attack, reconnaissance, and stealth missions. Matt is also at the top of the pyramid of a group of "A-gamers."

On one occasion Matt and I planned to fly from Mesa, Arizona down to Tucson to watch Aaron fly in the first Thunderbird show of the season, performed for the Air Force personnel stationed at Davis-Monthan Air Force Base. We'd be flying in an old Korean War-era fighter trainer, a T-28 "B" Model, affectionately called "The Trojan," which I've owned and flown for the last twelve years.

After spending some time doing the preflight and walk around, we climbed up on the wing to start getting strapped in. Like most fighter pilots of today, Matt didn't have any "round engine prop-time." Despite his thousands of hours of jet time, his combat experience, and his obvious expertise—this was an entirely new experience for him.

He listened intently during the preflight, asking relevant questions, and was genuinely interested in the background and flying character-istics of a piece of aviation history. As he was strapping into the parachute, I began explaining the egress procedure, should we have to bail out.

Mind you, I've never had to bail out of a plane and have never parachuted. The only time I'll ever bail out is if we're on fire. Save for that, I'm flying it to the ground. Bailing out of the T-28 is reported to be easy: blow off the canopy using a compressed nitrogen charge, unplug the communication cord attached to your helmet, roll the plane inverted, unbuckle your belt, and let Newton take care of the rest.

I was explaining the procedures in detail to Matt. About halfway through my monologue, it occurred to me that I wasn't sure if Air Force pilots, as part of their training, had to actually skydive. (They don't. They're towed behind a vehicle until they get to about five hundred feet, then are released and parachute to the ground so they can experience a landing).

About the time I was explaining how to pull the rip cord after clearing the plane, I stopped and asked Matt if he'd ever jumped. He flashed a shy smile and remarked, "Well, if we jump today, it will be my 762nd time. I was part of the Air Force Academy demonstration sky dive team."

I replied, "Okay then, here's how we're going to do it. I'm going to watch you, and do everything you do!"

What's so remarkable is that both Matt and Aaron have more to boast about than most of us. Yet, they don't spend one second trying to impress anyone, not even when given the obvious opportunity from a poser like me who was trying to explain how to jump out of an aircraft. The "real deals" don't need to boast; their actions and backgrounds speak for themselves.

Fragile—Handle with Care

Ego driven, insecure individuals can't bear to crack the thin veneer of their egos and thus won't venture into the unknown. In other words, they won't push the envelope. It's only when you push the envelope that you discover your limits. Without raising the bar or pushing the envelope, you'll likely never fail at much and thus never get to make lasting contributions.

What individuals with huge egos don't realize is that failure is a gift. We'll talk more about it in the next chapter.

───────── FOOD FOR THOUGHT ─────────

- Reading and learning about others reveals the degree and scope of their accomplishments and how they've handled both success and failure.

- Count the number of times in a day you find yourself telling others about your accomplishments and then work on decreasing that number.

- Remind yourself that having a fragile ego ultimately prevents you from taking risks and that failing to take calculated risks leads to stagnation.

IN OTHER WORDS

Egotism is the source and summary of all faults and miseries.
~ Thomas Carlyle

*Our own self-love draws a thick veil between us
and our faults.*
~ Lord Chesterfield

*One may understand the cosmos, but never the ego;
the self is more distant than any star.*
~ Gilbert Keith Chesterton

A self-made man? Yes, and worships his creator.
~ Henry Austin Clapp

*A person all wrapped up in himself generally makes
a pretty small package.*
~ E. Joseph Cossman

*The worst disease which can afflict business executives in their
work is not, as popularly supposed, alcoholism; it's egotism.*
~ Harold S. Geneen

*You have an ego—a consciousness of being an individual.
But that doesn't mean that you are to worship yourself, to
think constantly of yourself, and to live entirely for self.*
~ Billy Graham

*In all that surrounds him the egotist sees
only the frame of his own portrait.*
~ Jean Petit-Senn

Egotism is the glue with which you get stuck on yourself.
~ Dan Post

Avoid having your ego so close to your position
that when your position falls your ego goes with it."
~ Colin Powell

As long as you set yourself up
as a little God to which you must be loyal,
how can you hope to find inward peace?
~ A.W. Tozer

No man has learned the meaning of life
until he has surrendered his ego
to the service of his fellow men.
~ Beran Wolfe

Fail Fast: The Gift of Failure

It's not your IQ, it's your FQ, your failure quotient.
Most of us handle failure in one of several ways.
We blame it on somebody else, we deny it happened, we become
embarrassed by it or we totally lose confidence and give up.
You have a fifth avenue and that's to rise from your ashes.

~ Dale Brown

Failure a gift? What a strange combination: the words "gift" and "failure" linked together in one brief statement! At first glance, it seems completely contradictory. How can there be anything positive about failure? Is there really a way to "rise from your ashes" of failure, as aviator and best-selling author Dale Brown suggested?

Gifts, of course, are generally positive. We give and receive them on happy occasions. There are wedding gifts, anniversary gifts, birthday gifts, Christmas gifts, thank you gifts. They generally convey love, appreciation, or gratitude. Of course there are other gifts, less tangible, but even more important: our time, talents, encouragement, compassion, kindness, and love.

Failure, on the other hand, suggests a much different story. Let's look at some of the synonyms for failure: default, delinquency, breakdown, shortage, deterioration, bankruptcy and—in the vernacular—we have fiasco, tango-uniform (tits up), delta-uniform (dick up), flop, washout, flameout, bomb, and bust.

We become acquainted with failure early in life. Students fail exams, and it's unlikely that dad or mom, when presented with a report card showing Ds and Fs, will bestow any gifts—believe me, they don't! Candidates fail to win elections; everything from automobile brakes to Broadway plays routinely fail; people fail to pay their taxes; hearts and lungs and livers and eyesight and numerous other body parts all fail all the time.

In 1929, many banks failed, resulting in years of economic chaos and depression. And surely none of the thousands of entrepreneurs whose businesses fail annually would call such failure "a gift."

Throughout our lives, we've been conditioned to connect failure with something negative. Failure, however, need not be either fatal or final. There is indeed a "fifth avenue" out of failure. In that same theme, John Keats, the nineteenth century English poet, called failure "the highway to success," and well-known motivational author and speaker Zig Ziglar described it as "a detour, not a dead-end street."

You may have seen this quote by Walter Brunell: "Failure is the tuition you pay for success." I've paid a lot of tuition over the years, both in and out of formal schooling. Despite all the education, I've been a failure again and again—thank God. Fortunately for me, I keep finding new and innovative ways to fail!

An Early Start

My gift of failure started early. As noted previously, despite being tall and coming from a family that encouraged sports, I never really excelled at anything where coordination, speed, or strength mattered, thus relegating me to events like curling and badminton. My sister, however, was a very competitive swimmer, as well as a straight "A" student. Fortunately I was adopted, so I could genuinely claim some form of genetic malady (I still do). In fact, genetics haunt me to this day.

A few years ago, I was speaking to about five hundred physicians on the subject of entrepreneurism and intelligent failures. After the talk, I had a number of people come by to ask questions. One gentleman, a dermatologist from Indiana who waited until the line cleared out, said to me, "Mind if I tell you something?" I responded, "Of course not." To which he said, "You are very striking."

I was taken aback by what I interpreted as a "pick up line." He must have seen the surprised look on my face because his next comment was, "No really, you are quite handsome." Just when I thought I was going to have to claim rampant heterosexuality, he said, "Get your growth hormone checked, I think you have a pituitary tumor." So even today, genetics still haunt me!

After a particularly bad report card, I remember telling my parents, "When it matters, I *will* get it right." My parents weren't buying any of it, because they'd become used to my dismal academic showings, but on this particular report card, I set the bar incredibly low.

As I described in painful detail in Chapter 1, this sort of non-success in academia and sports continued throughout high school. Retrospectively, my lack of any measure of success through that part of my life actually saved me. Many of my peer group who were the outliers in high school burned out early. Things came easily for them and, when challenged, they simply fell apart. They simply weren't used to having to work hard. Their past success made them feel entitled. They felt they simply deserved to be successful because of who they were and what they *once* accomplished.

When I finally got my act together by working harder than I'd ever worked in the past, I knew I'd actually earned it— nothing came easily. But for my repeated failures, I wouldn't have known or appreciated the belief in self that comes from getting up over and over again, dusting yourself off, and pressing on. I can say with certainty that I've learned far more from my failures than from any small success.

Going into Business[es]

With my newly discovered burst of self-confidence, I decided to launch my business career. But where to start? I'd once entertained thoughts of owning a restaurant. I knew nothing about restaurant operations, so I thought it would be less risky to start out with hot dog stands. I bought five of them, and in the winter in Phoenix, Arizona, they did really well—in the summer, however, not so much.

The hot dog stands were a huge failure—but that didn't stop me. Since then I've started, or invested in and owned, or continue to own:

- More hot dog stands—and an autopsy business (I tried not to confuse the two)
- A helicopter training and leasing company
- An Internet company selling medical slides (in 1997)
- A production company for a TV pilot
- An Emergency Department staffing company with a number of hospital ED management contracts
- A medical billing company
- A digital x-ray supply company
- A TV show, *Your Health A to Z*
- A radio show, *Top Doc*
- A company which sends HIPPA compliant radiology images via the Internet
- A wine bar/restaurant
- A law firm
- A laser hair removal business
- An Internet search engine company for urgent care centers
- A radiology imaging interpretation company

- A business called *PASS*, which evaluated and rehabilitated doctors with personality disorders and predicted which physicians will be sued for malpractice

- A company which allowed consumers to send out and receive bids for their health care or their animal's vet needs

In 1993, I launched what became *NextCare Urgent Care*, which at one point was one of the largest privately held urgent care companies in the country. Two physician partners and I started *NextCare* with $10,000. One partner bailed out after two weeks and the other is still a stockholder, but didn't want to take on more debt or risk. I didn't take any salary for 11 years and worked about 80 hours a week on top of practicing emergency medicine.

Sadly, and I suppose thankfully, I left some of my less memorable ideas on the design table. A few of them which didn't stick include:

- A company called *Dead TV*, to produce and air video obituaries on the Internet and cable TV—and a TV pilot called *Dancing with the Disabled*

- A men's sportswear line called *A-Game*—and a women's sportswear line called *Such!*

- A wine aerator to bubble oxygen into red wine to shorten the breathing process

Oops!

Until sometime after *NextCare* was in existence, one common denominator fit a lot of my earlier business ventures, at least initially: I didn't know what the hell I was doing! Prior to earning an MBA, the only business class I'd ever taken was typing (which I failed) in high school. Hence, I operated on a purely gut level instinct and made lots and lots of mistakes.

For example: my snow shoveling and grass cutting abilities nearly got my parents sued; my candles melted without lighting; and my chocolate tasted oddly of wax. (I used the same molds.) Who knew? I once ran out of gas in my ambulance just after I'd dropped a patient with an abdominal aortic aneurysm off at the hospital.

Once I got very hungry while flying a helicopter and landed out in the middle of the reservation, right next to a small Indian Fry Bread stand. How could I have known the five-gallon container of powdered sugar wasn't covered? Those poor people wound up looking like ghosts as a large plume of powdered sugar rose from the roofless stand.

While working at the hot dog stand, after spending all day in class and all night in the ED, I saw this guy staring at me in Home Depot while I had about fifteen people waiting for their hot dogs. Every time I looked up, he was still staring at me. Finally, he walked over and said, "Don't I know you from somewhere?" I had no idea who he was and told him so. Undeterred, he went on, "Wait, don't you work in the emergency department of St. Luke's Hospital?"

I was mortified! He continued, "You sewed up my foot last week and you left some glass in it!" Struggling to regain my composure, I said, "That's why I'm selling hot dogs now."

I co-wrote, co-produced, and "co-starred" in a TV pilot to be called "Your Health A-Z." I'd never really done any acting, so I went to a famous ex-soap opera star who gave acting lessons. After a few lessons, during which I would have to read little scripts with her, she told me she wanted me to read some lines in a voice like I was trying to seduce her. Instead, I quoted a line from the film "Zoolander," when Jon Voight says to Ben Stiller: "Damn it, Derek, I'm a coal miner, not a professional film and television actor."

She said: "Are you trying to be funny? 'Cause you're not. In fact, you're so boring I need to make a pot of coffee just to drive home." Thinking she traveled a long distance, I asked, "How far away do you live?" She said, "About a mile."

Not surprisingly, that was our last meeting. Consequently, she never told me that men should *not* wear shorts on television because, when you're sitting down, low angle camera shots tend to enter the domain of the Spice Channel. Needless to say, the show's ratings went way down and one kind viewer wanted to start a nonprofit fund for me—use your imagination.

Lessons Learned

But I learned—and learning is the key. The point is this: if you approach failure as simply a hurdle to jump or an event from which you can learn, failing's not so bad. In fact, it may lead to your next success. If you're willing to learn, willing to risk, and willing to either conduct serious reflection or accept criticism from others, failure is a necessary ingredient of success.

Failure has many wonderful and valuable lessons to teach us, so let's look at a few examples of successful people who learned that failure is *not* a dead-end street, but just a detour along the highway to success.

A Boy Called Ted

The son of German immigrants, Ted was born in Springfield, Massachusetts in 1904. He had a comfortable childhood. He attended Dartmouth College and was editor-in-chief of its humor magazine, until a drinking party cost him that position. After college he traveled to Europe and briefly attended Oxford University before dropping out and continuing his European wanderings.

After returning to the U.S., Ted worked successfully for many years in the advertising business and as an editorial cartoonist, while nurturing his dream of becoming a children's book author. His first such book was initially rejected by 27 publishers, but he refused to give up. When it was finally published, it became the first of 44 children's books, which he both wrote and illustrated.

During his highly successful career he received many honors, including two Academy awards, two Emmy awards, a Peabody award, and a

Pulitzer Prize. His name: Theodor S. Geisel. That middle initial stands, of course, for Seuss, which was also his mother's maiden name.

Those magical Dr. Seuss books have been translated into more than a dozen languages, with combined sales of more than two hundred million copies. The world of children's literature would be a less happy place, except for this man who refused to take "No" for an answer, not even 27 times.

Joanne's Story

Joanne was the older of two daughters born to a London couple who met and married when they were 19. When Joanne was a teenager, her mother became seriously ill and a few years later, at age 45, she died. "It was a terrible time," Joanne recalled, leaving her with "a literal pain in my heart." Still grieving, she moved to Portugal, where she'd gotten a job teaching English. Soon after, she married a Portuguese man and gave birth to a daughter.

After a divorce, she returned home with her three-month-old daughter. It was a difficult and depressing time for her, a single mother who was unemployed and living on welfare. Whenever she found a few spare minutes, she worked on a novel which had been burning inside her for years. When she finally finished it, she managed to capture the interest of a literary agent, who agreed to represent her.

For a year, her manuscript went from publisher to publisher, only to be rejected time and again. Then, finally, came the phone call from her agent to tell her it had been accepted. Yet there was still one small issue to be resolved. Fearing that using her first name might limit the book's appeal to all audiences, the publisher asked that she use the initials of her first and middle names, instead of Joanne.

However, she'd never been given a middle name, so she decided to add the name of a recently deceased and much loved grandmother. That grandmother's first name was Kathleen. Not long afterward, Joanne's first book was published.

On June 5, 2008, by then a billionaire, J.K. Rowling was the featured speaker at Harvard University's commencement ceremonies. During that speech, she said: "I'm not going to stand here and tell you that failure is fun. That period of my life was a dark one... you may never fail on the scale that I did, but some failure in life is inevitable, unless you live so cautiously that you might as well not have lived at all—in which case, you fail by default."

The Immigrants' Son

On May 10, 1899, Frederick Austerlitz, the son of Austrian immigrants, was born in Omaha, Nebraska. As children, Frederick and his sister Adele began singing and dancing in vaudeville shows and continued to do so for many years.

A vaudeville show featured a variety of entertainers—including singers, dancers, comedians, ventriloquists, jugglers, magicians, and others—who would appear on stage in rapid-fire succession during shows lasting up to twelve hours. Many successful stage and movie careers were launched in vaudeville theaters across America.

When his sister quit in 1932 to get married, Frederick, now in his early 30s, headed to Hollywood to make his fortune. The movie industry was booming and two of the major studios were RKO and MGM. Frederick signed a contract with RKO, which promptly loaned him to MGM to appear in a film titled *Dancing Lady*.

His MGM screen test didn't go so well. The director conducting the test wrote this note: "Can't act, can't sing, slightly bald, can dance a little." Nevertheless, he was given a supporting role in *Dancing Lady*, starring Joan Crawford and Clark Gable. But were you to check the list of cast members for that film, you'd search unsuccessfully for the name Frederick Austerlitz. By that time, he'd become Fred Astaire.

Back at RKO, Astaire became famous first as a dancer teamed with Ginger Rogers, another early Hollywood star. Later, as his fame grew, he also successfully took on singing and straight dramatic roles, although his greatest fame came as a dancer. He is still considered by many as America's most famous dancer.

One of Astaire's earliest films with Ginger Rogers was titled *Swing Time*, which featured a song titled, "Pick Yourself Up," to which the pair danced magnificently (check it out on YouTube). The music was written by famed composer Jerome Kern, but it was Dorothy Fields' lyrics that express the primary message of this chapter probably better than I ever could.

The song ends with these words: "Will you remember the famous men / Who had to fall and rise again? / So take a deep breath / Pick yourself up / Dust yourself off / Start all over again."

In case you're wondering what happened to that note the MGM casting director wrote, Fred Astaire kept it prominently displayed in his Beverly Hills home, reminding him of the roadblock he faced on his journey to success.

Something in Common

These are not isolated stories. For the vast majority of people who became successful in whatever area they excelled in, there were no easy roads. They have a common trait that without it, things like the battery, the electric light bulb, heart transplantation, human flight, the personal computer, and countless other leaps in technology and science would have never happened.

The wisdom gained through failure is both incontrovertible and invaluable. Despite this, neither people nor organizations seem to handle it well. Harvard Professor Amy Edmondson wrote, "We are programmed at an early age to think that failure is bad. That belief prevents organizations [and individuals] from effectively learning from their missteps." The phrase, "Fail fast so that you succeed sooner," is a good mantra for those who are testing possible hypotheses while they are "building the wings as they fly."

Failure is inevitable in today's complex society. The key is to simply fail fast, fail intelligently, learn, and press on. When you feel you can no longer go on and you want to quit, realize that you may be just a few inches/days/dollars from success. Keep turning the pages to learn what these successful people know!

───── FOOD FOR THOUGHT ─────

- Failing fast means you're growing quickly.

- All successful people were failures along their journey—the only difference is that they learned and persevered.

- If it was easy, everyone would do it, and then it wouldn't be an accomplishment, it would be an expectation.

───── IN OTHER WORDS ─────

Failure is just another way to learn
how to do something right.
~ Marian Wright Edelman

An inventor fails 999 times, and if he succeeds once,
he's in. He treats his failures simply as practice shots.
~ Charles F. Kettering

Failure will never overtake me
if my determination to succeed is strong enough.
~ Og Mandino

There are always reasons for giving up.
There is no such thing as failure
except to those who accept and believe in failure.
~ Orison Swett Marden

*Remember there are two benefits of failure. First, if you do
fail, you learn what doesn't work; and second, the failure gives
you an opportunity to try a new approach.*
~ Roger von Oech

*Most people give up just when they're about to achieve success.
They quit on the one yard line. They give up at the last minute
of the game, one foot from a winning touchdown.*
~ H. Ross Perot

*He who hopes to avoid all failure and misfortune
is trying to live in a fairyland; the wise man readily accepts
failures as a part of life and builds a philosophy
to meet them and make the most of them.*
~ Wilferd A. Peterson

*We learn far more about ourselves in our failures than in
our successes. Failure is the greatest teacher of all. Failure
dramatizes where we are yet incomplete, and points the way
to wholeness. So failure may be the future signaling to us.*
~ Robert A. Raines

*Failure is not failure to meet your goal.
Real failure is failure to reach as high as you possibly can.
No man will ever truly know that he has succeeded until he
experiences an apparent failure.*
~ Robert Schuller

*We learn wisdom from failure much more than from success. We
often discover what will do, by finding out what will not do.*
~ Samuel Smiles

*Forget about the consequences of failure. Failure is only a tempo-
rary change in direction to set you straight for your next success.*
~ Denis Waitley

CHAPTER

Persistence: Press On!

Nothing in the world can take the place of persistence.
Talent will not; nothing is more common than unsuccessful men with
talent. Genius will not; unrewarded genius is almost a Proverb.
Education will not; the world is full of educated failures. Persistence
and determination alone are omnipotent. The slogan 'Press On' has
solved and always will solve the problems of the human heart.

~ Calvin Coolidge

The above words, spoken nearly a century ago by the 30th President of the United States, have long been favorites of mine. They epitomize a core principle on which our nation was founded, and on which it has been shaped. Call it what you will—persistence, determination, tenacity, perseverance—it's the quality of pressing on toward a goal, no matter what obstacles or difficulties may stand in the way.

This was brought home to me in a special way a few years ago when I attended the annual conference of the American College of Emergency Physicians, held that year in Boston. While there, along with learning (and relearning) some emergency medicine, I had the chance to walk along the Freedom Trail and enhance my understanding of our battle for independence.

What continually amazes me is how fortunate we were to actually succeed. Many times the only thing which turned the tide and saved the day was the perseverance of our founders. Many historians consider the Siege of Boston (starting after the battles of Lexington and Concord) to be the beginning of the Revolutionary War.

During the siege, militiamen surrounded Boston, attempting to prevent the British Army, which was garrisoned within Boston, from receiving supplies. To fortify his army's position and prevent the British Navy from supplying the British Army, General George Washington sent a 25-year-old bookseller named Henry Knox to bring heavy cannons that had been captured at Fort Ticonderoga in New York all the way to Dorchester Heights, Massachusetts, which overlooked Boston's harbor.

Over the wet and freezing winter of 1775-76, Knox and his small group moved 60 tons of artillery—by boat, horse-drawn sledges (which they built), and sheer perseverance—300 miles along snow-packed trails, across two semi-frozen rivers, and through forests and swamps, to the Boston area. It took them 56 days, averaging about five-and-a-half miles a day, to get those 120,000 pounds of artillery to their destination. It was a remarkable feat in the face of daunting obstacles.

Historian Victor Brooks called it "one of the most stupendous feats of logistics" of the entire war. Ultimately, the effectiveness of these cannons marked the turning point which eventually forced the British out of Boston.

Knox went on to serve with distinction in the Continental Army and rose through the ranks to become its youngest major general. Later, he served as the nation's first Secretary of War and went on to champion the rights of Native Americans. Most importantly, his extraordinary accomplishments paved the way for our eventual independence.

Too Dumb to Quit?

In 1993, I started a company initially called Arizona Family and

Urgent Care (AFUC), on a shoestring. I literally worked day and night to get it up and running. During its early stage, one partner backed out and another one said he didn't want to take on any more risk.

I pressed on and we were actually making headway when the bank called our loan and put us in the "workout" division. At the time I thought this was great because I liked to work out. Then I learned that this was the area of the bank where bad loans were handled. The bank could have called the note at any time, which means it would have taken over and seized all our assets.

So we triple mortgaged our house and finally switched banks. When I went back and asked why the man who was our "workout banker" didn't simply call the note, he told me it was because he never heard "defeat in your voice." We eventually changed the name to *NextCare* when I heard an employee answer the phone, "Hello, thank you for calling "Aw-Fuc!" I served as chairman and CEO of *NextCare* until 2010, by which time it had grown from a single clinic to 58 clinics in six states with an annualized revenue of nearly $100 million dollars.

Now maybe I'm just too dumb to quit, but remember: you're never beaten until you admit it. For those of us who get into fights, the worst people to fight with are those who are too dumb or too tenacious to quit because they just keep coming back.

A Shining Example

America's history is replete with the stories of men and women whose "press on" and "never quit" attitudes are shining examples of the determination and the persevering spirit on which our nation was built. Among my favorites is Theodore Roosevelt, the President of the United States from 1901 to 1909.

Although he was one of the most colorful and popular men to have ever served in that capacity, Roosevelt was far more than a political figure. He was—among other things—an adventurer, an historian, a hunter, a naturalist, an orator, an explorer, and an author. His prodigious literary output includes 26 books, more than a thousand magazine articles, and thousands of speeches and letters.

Examples of Roosevelt's perseverance abound. In 1912, as he was about to begin a speech, he was shot in the chest by a would-be assassin. Undeterred, he proceeded to deliver his speech after commenting to his audience: "Ladies and gentlemen, I don't know if you fully understand but I have just been shot, but it takes more than that to kill a Bull Moose." With blood seeping through his clothing, he spoke for 90 minutes before being taken to a hospital. The bullet would remain in his chest for the rest of his life.

In 1913, downcast following a rare political defeat, Roosevelt wanted to get away from Washington and accepted an invitation to speak in Argentina. While in South America, he joined forces with some Brazilian explorers to navigate a thousand-mile-long tributary of the Amazon River named the Rio da Duvida, the River of Doubt. It was a dangerous journey, one which nearly killed Roosevelt. Nevertheless, the team overcame one obstacle after another, successfully mapping the entire length of the Rio da Duvida. In recognition of that amazing feat and of the courage and tenacity of its leader, Brazilian officials changed the name of that river to Rio Roosevelt.

The story of that journey was told by author Candice Millard in her 2005 book, *The River of Doubt*. In the prologue this is how she described Roosevelt: "Each time he encountered an obstacle, he responded with more vigor, more energy, more raw determination. Each time he faced personal tragedy or weakness, he found his strength not in the sympathy of others, but in the harsh ordeal of unfamiliar new challenges and harsh adventure."

Theodore Roosevelt might as well have been describing himself when he wrote these words: "It is not the critic who counts, not the one who points out how the strong man stumbled or how the doer of deeds might have done better. The credit belongs to the man who is actually in the arena, whose face is marred with sweat and dust and blood; who strives valiantly; who errs and comes short again and again; who knows the great enthusiasms, the great devotions, and spends himself in a worthy cause; who, if he wins, knows the triumph of high achievement; and who, if he fails, at least fails while daring greatly, so that his place shall never be with those cold and timid souls who know neither victory nor defeat."

From Braces to Races

The woman whose story follows had no aspirations to be a role model. "I don't consciously try to be a role model," she said, "so I don't know if I am or not. That's for others to decide." After reading her story, I'm sure you'll agree that she proved to be an outstanding one, inspiring others to press on, no matter what obstacles they faced.

Born prematurely in 1940 in the segregated South, the twentieth of 22 children in a desperately poor family, there was nothing about this tiny four-and-a-half-pound baby girl to suggest future greatness. She was a sickly child, stricken with a variety of illnesses, including scarlet fever, pneumonia, and then polio, which required her to wear leg braces. The doctors told her she would never be able to walk without them and her future seemed bleak.

But inside that frail young body was a persevering spirit; she was determined to prove the doctors wrong. Later in her life, she made this comment: "My doctors told me I would never walk again. My mother told me I would. I believed my mother." At age nine she shed those braces and began—hesitantly at first—to walk, and then to run. She went on to become a basketball star in high school and then a world-class runner, first as a star sprinter on the Tennessee State University track team and then as an Olympic gold medalist.

Her name was Wilma Rudolph. In 1956, at the age of 16 and still in high school, she was selected as a member of the United States Olympic Team and helped her relay team win a bronze medal in Melbourne, Australia.

But her greatest Olympic triumphs came four years later, during the 1960 Games in Rome. She began by winning the gold medal in the 100-meter dash and followed it by winning the 200-meter dash, setting a new Olympic record in the process. Finally, she earned a third gold medal as a member of the world-record-setting relay team.

This once sickly child, told she would never walk, thus became the first American woman ever to win three gold medals in a single Olympics. Nicknamed "The Black Gazelle" and "The Black Pearl," Wilma Rudolph became a worldwide celebrity, acclaimed as "the world's fastest woman," and was named "Female Athlete of the Year" by The Associated Press.

Despite the adversity she had to overcome as a child, for which she clearly deserved enormous credit, she was always quick to acknowledge that many others played significant roles in her success. "No matter what accomplishments you make," she once said, "somebody helps you."

After retiring from running, she spent the rest of her life helping others. She became a teacher, coach, and motivational speaker and was appointed by the U.S. State Department as a Goodwill Ambassador in Africa. She also played a significant role in striking down segregation laws in her hometown of Clarksville, Tennessee by refusing to participate in any tributes to her unless they were open to all, regardless of the color of their skin.

With all her athletic achievements, Rudolph claimed that her greatest accomplishment was starting a foundation that sponsored athletic outreach programs for underprivileged youth in the ghettoes of more than a dozen major U.S. cities. Until her untimely death of brain cancer at the age of 54, she continued her active involvement in the lives of others.

She was an inspiration to thousands of people whose lives she touched. "Never underestimate the power of dreams and the influence of the human spirit," she wrote, adding these words: "The potential for greatness lives within each of us."

Wilma Rudolph achieved that greatness, not for her athletic performance, but because of her tenacious spirit and refusal to accept defeat in any aspect of her life.

An Unlikely Hero

Chances are you've never heard the amazing story of a man named Cliff Young, but he's a legend half a world away—in Australia, the Land Down Under.

The legend began in 1983, as the inaugural foot race from Sydney to Melbourne was about to get underway. It was an ambitious undertaking, covering a distance of 875 kilometers, or more than 540 miles. That's the equivalent of running nearly 21 complete marathons—in a row! To put it in perspective, that would be similar to running from New York City to Raleigh, North Carolina or from Los Angeles to Reno.

About 150 superbly conditioned athletes had signed up to participate in what was expected to be a six-day event. So race officials were taken aback when Cliff Young showed up and requested an entry form, saying he was ready to go. This 61-year-old, wearing overalls and galoshes over his work boots, didn't exactly fit the picture of a world-class distance runner.

Convinced the man was either crazy or that it was some sort of publicity stunt, officials told him he couldn't run. But Cliff Young was determined to compete. He'd spent his life on his family's sprawling 2,000-acre farm, with 2,000 head of sheep. His family was poor and could afford neither horses nor tractors, he explained. Whenever the storms rolled in, Cliff's job was to start running and round up the sheep. It was no small task. Sometimes, he said it would take two or three days of running to finish the job.

It sounded like a totally improbable tale but, reluctantly, the officials allowed him to enter, hoping he wouldn't drop dead during the race. Off they went, and the world-class athletes were quickly out of sight, leaving old Cliff way behind, shuffling along in his galoshes. But no one had thought to explain to him that the race plan called for eighteen hours of running, followed by six hours of rest, so he just kept right on shuffling along. After all, it took perseverance to round up all those sheep when the storms came; there was never time to take even a short break.

By the fifth day, Cliff had caught and passed them all, easily winning the race, and becoming a national hero. It was the centuries-old Aesop's Fable, *The Tortoise and The Hare*, brought to life. Ironically, many of these super athletes who had first sneered at Cliff's peculiar shuffling style later adopted it themselves, finding it better suited for extremely long distances.

But there's more to this Cliff Young story—a lot more. He continued to complete in ultra-marathon events, training for them by running 30 kilometers (18.6 miles) a day on his farm. Then, at age 76, he announced that he would try and become the oldest man to run completely around Australia, which is roughly the size of the continental United States.

The distance: 16,000 kilometers, or nearly 10,000 miles! It was an extraordinarily ambitious undertaking but, unfortunately, through no fault of his own, he was unable to achieve his goal. His only permanent crew member, who drove the support vehicle and provided Cliff with food and water, became ill during the run and Cliff had to stop.

Cliff was very disappointed about having to quit the run after *only* 6,520 kilometers, or more than 4,000 miles. He'd been running for nearly three months, averaging the equivalent of about one-and-a-half marathons a day—at age 76!

But it was more than his amazing feats of perseverance and courage that made Cliff Young a great man. He was an inspiration to millions and a great encourager of younger runners. In 2004, the year after his death at age 81, the organizers of the race where he first gained fame permanently changed its name to the Cliff Young Australian Six Day Race in his honor and memory.

There are two other parts to the Cliff Young story. When he entered that first race in 1983, it never occurred to him that there was any prize money involved, and so he was quite surprised to learn he had won $10,000, a huge sum for that poor farmer. However, instead of keeping it, he gave $2,000 to each of the five runners who had finished most closely behind him.

And the main reason he was so disappointed at having to quit his run around Australia was that he had undertaken it to raise money for homeless children!

The Bottom Line

Give me people like Henry Knox, Theodore Roosevelt, Wilma Rudolph, and Cliff Young—men and women who won't quit, who have great attitudes, and who refuse to let obstacles or setbacks cause them to abandon their dreams. I'll hire them in a second and they *will be* very successful.

Here's the bottom line: if it was easy, everyone would do it. With ordinary talent and extraordinary perseverance, all things are attainable. I relish the challenging opportunities. The higher the bar to clear, the more difficult it is for everyone else as well.

It's your choice. You can live in the world of regrets, the world of "If only …," of "I coulda, shoulda, woulda…" or you can follow the examples of those whose stories I've shared.

Perseverance, determination, tenacity, persistence — or whatever term you choose to describe it — is the "secret sauce" which separates the achievers from the wishful thinkers. Don't let regrets replace your dreams. Follow this advice from the pen of Langston Hughes, the famous African-American poet and author: "Hold fast to dreams / For if dreams die / Life is a broken-winged bird / That cannot fly."

FOOD FOR THOUGHT

- A 61-year-old running 540 miles; a man getting shot in the chest and then giving a speech; a child in leg braces becoming an Olympic Champion! If they, despite their obstacles, can accomplish such great feats, what can you do?

- I've seen the profound angst in the eyes of dying patients; you don't want to find yourself on your deathbed saying, "If only."

IN OTHER WORDS

You cannot keep determined people from success. If you place stumbling blocks in their way, they will use them for stepping-stones and climb to new heights.
~ Mary Kay Ash

Most of the important things in the world have been accomplished by people who have kept on trying when there seemed to be no hope at all.
~ Dale Carnegie

Do not quit! Hundreds of times I have watched people throw in the towel at the one-yard line while someone else comes along and makes a fortune by just going that extra yard.
~ E. Joseph Cossman

Lightning rarely strikes. Instead, achievement is often the result of stepwise progress, of doing something increasingly difficult until you get the result you seek.
~ Seth Godin

Big shots are only little shots who keep on shooting.
~ Christopher Morley

I'm convinced that about half of what separates the successful entrepreneurs from the non-successful ones is pure perseverance.

~ Steve Jobs

Keep on going and the chances are you will stumble on something, perhaps when you are least expecting it. I have never heard of anyone stumbling on something sitting down.

~ Charles F. Kettering

Perseverance is a great element of success.
If you only knock long enough and loud enough at the gate, you are sure to wake somebody.

~ Henry Wadsworth Longfellow

Have the dogged determination to follow through to achieve your goal; regardless of circumstances or whatever other people say, think, or do.

~ Paul J. Meyer

A steadfast soul, holding steadily to a dream ideal, plus a sturdy will determined to succeed in any venture, can make any dream come true. Use your mind and your will. They work together for you beautifully if you'll only give them a chance.

~ B.N. Mills

I do not think there is any other quality so essential to success of any kind as the quality of perseverance. It overcomes almost everything, even nature.

~ John D. Rockefeller

Far better is it to dare mighty things, to win glorious triumphs, even though checkered by failure . . . than to rank with those poor spirits who neither enjoy nor suffer much, because they live in a gray twilight that knows not victory nor defeat.

~ Theodore Roosevelt

*There is no chance, no destiny, no fate
that can circumvent or hinder or control
the firm resolve of a determined soul.*
~ Ella Wheeler Wilcox

CHAPTER

Preparation: When the Wind Blows

Success at almost anything doesn't just happen.
In almost every area of your life,
the more you prepare, the better the result will be.
~ Joel H. Weldon

There's an old tale about a wealthy farmer whose large dairy farm covered several hundred acres along Maine's Atlantic coast. Because of the sudden and severe storms that would blow in frequently from the ocean, the farmer had trouble keeping hired hands. As soon as one of these storms would hit, they'd be on their way to safer places inland, leaving farm equipment and frightened cattle out in the storms.

Then one day a young man showed up at the farmer's front door looking for work. As the farmer began asking him about his experience as a farmhand, the young man would simply answer: "I can sleep when the wind blows." The farmer had no idea what he meant, but the last of his helpers had taken to his heels a week or so earlier, and the farmer was desperate, so he hired him on the spot.

A few nights later the farmer was awakened by a roaring storm that had suddenly blown in off the coast in all its fury. Hurrying to find his helper, he found him sound asleep in his bunk. "Wake up! Wake up!"

he yelled, but the young man simply said as he rolled over, "I can sleep when the wind blows." No matter how many times the farmer tried to get him out of bed, the answer was always the same.

Angry and frustrated, and determined to fire the young man as soon as morning arrived, the farmer rushed out into the storm. The first thing he noticed was that all the equipment had been tied down and covered with tarpaulins. Running to the barn, he found all the cows safe in their stalls. All the doors and shutters had been secured. Suddenly, the farmer remembered the young man's words. Understanding now what he meant, he too was able to go back to bed and sleep, while the wind kept blowing.

I can hardly imagine a profession, a career, or even an entry-level job where preparation isn't at least advantageous, ranging on up to important, critical, indispensable, and even life-saving. As a physician and as a pilot, I can't imagine how anyone can consider entrusting their safety, their health, and even their lives to someone in either of those fields who isn't merely competent but is fully prepared to meet their needs, no matter what surprises or potential emergencies may be at hand—someone who can sleep when the wind blows.

Where's the Flight Deck?

If you're sitting on a commercial airliner that's preparing for takeoff and happen to overhear the captain asking that question, it probably wouldn't do a whole lot for your peace of mind. An unlikely situation? Sure it is, but I heard of one case where it could have happened.

Years ago, a senior captain of one of the major airlines was preparing to fly a Boeing 747 from Los Angeles to Seoul, Korea. It would be the first time he'd ever even set foot on a 747, much less flown one, and had a full load of passengers counting on him.

As he was making his way through a hangar to board the flight, he spotted another 747 on which a crew was doing some maintenance, so he decided to climb aboard and look around. Walking forward through the main cabin, he reached the front of the plane, but there was no flight deck or cockpit to be found. That's when he learned from a nearby mechanic that the cockpit on the 747 is on the upper deck.

Imagine if that had been the plane scheduled for Korea. Walking up the aisle of that fully loaded plane and having to ask one of the flight crew—or worse, one of the passengers—how to get to the cockpit would likely have triggered a stampede toward the exits.

But was that pilot unprepared to fly that plane? Certainly not! He'd spent many hours in a flight simulator, which was an exact replica of the 747 cockpit. He'd already learned everything he needed to know about flying that plane and had dealt with extremely realistic simulations of just about every potential emergency. That training, combined with some 25,000 hours of flight time during his career, had him fully prepared to fly that aircraft (once he located the flight deck, of course).

Occasionally, before performing a spinal tap (inserting a long needle into the space where the spinal cord travels) I will remark, "I think this is how you do this—it's my first one." When I say that, I get some gauge on the person's level of engagement and certainly on his or her sense of humor. Does making this comment mean I'm unprepared? No, it means I have a sick sense of humor.

Last year, I was involved in a near fatal airplane crash. I was the passenger in the cockpit of a plane which crashed on takeoff. A pilot friend was flying when a gust of wind hit us right at the moment of takeoff from a mountain airstrip. The plane veered off the runway to the left and then back to the right before striking a hangar.

Luckily, the person in the backseat near the exit (also a pilot) kicked the door open a moment before impact. Otherwise, we'd have been trapped. The pilot adroitly swung the tail of the plane around just prior to impact and therefore avoided going head first into the hangar door. We were all able to jump out as the plane caught fire and then exploded. No one said a word during the event; it was as if we'd rehearsed for this moment. The three of us have been flying together for a number of years, and oddly enough, we talked through a couple of "what if" scenarios over dinner the night before. One of the scenarios we talked about was being trapped in a burning plane and how important it was to jettison the doors prior to impact.

Here's the bottom line: if you know what's coming, if you've thought about all the various permutations of what could happen, nothing surprises you because you've already been there—you've prepared.

An Important Tool

During my careers as a physician, attorney, and entrepreneur—and as a pilot—I've come to rely heavily on a relatively simple but highly effective tool to ensure that I'm thoroughly prepared to carry out my prescribed responsibilities, as well as to respond effectively should something unexpected occur. That tool is called a checklist—a significant asset, in a wide range of activities, to prepare to deliver positive results and prevent negative ones.

A pioneer and a champion in the cause of checklists in the world of medicine is surgeon and author Atul Gawande. In his 2009 book, *The Checklist Manifesto*, Doctor Gawande writes:

> We have accumulated stupendous know-how. We have put it in the hands of some of the most highly trained, highly skilled, and hardworking people in our society. And, with it, they have indeed accomplished extraordinary things. Nonetheless, that know-how is often unmanageable. Avoidable failures are common and persistent, not to mention demoralizing and frustrating, across many fields—from medicine to finance, business to government. And the reason is increasingly evident: the volume and complexity of what we know has exceeded our individual ability to deliver its benefits correctly, safely, or reliably. Knowledge has both saved us and burdened us.
>
> That means we need a different strategy for overcoming failure, one that builds on experience and takes advantage of the

knowledge people have but somehow also makes up for our inevitable human inadequacies. And there is such a strategy— though it will seem almost ridiculous in its simplicity, maybe even crazy to those of us who have spent years carefully developing even more advanced skills and technologies.

It is a checklist.

We probably don't think of them specifically as "checklists," but we use them regularly in a variety of ways. The outline for this book is a checklist, as is that grocery list on your refrigerator door. How many times have you had to make a second trip to the grocery store for an item on that list, which you'd forgotten to take with you the first time?

Want to get organized and make better use of your time? Nearly always, the first recommendation will be to keep a "to-do" list, and to check off each item as you complete it. Recipes are checklists, and so are budgets, Christmas card lists, and those written directions you keep in your car for your occasional visits to Great Aunt Maude's place out in the boonies. Simplicity indeed!

In his review of *The Checklist Manifesto*, best-selling and award-winning author Malcolm Gladwell writes: "Gawande is a gorgeous writer and storyteller, and the aims of this book are ambitious. Gawande thinks the modern world requires us to revisit what we mean by expertise: that experts need help, and that progress depends on experts having the humility to concede that they need help."

Two similar and tragic events involving private pilots based in the Phoenix area underscore the benefits of checklists and what can happen as a result of inadequate preparation. In both cases, the pilots realized—shortly after takeoff—that they had failed to secure doors. One radioed that he could take care of it himself and, thus distracted, he crashed his plane into the side of a building and was killed on impact.

The other pilot, on departing from San Diego, reported his problem and radioed that he was returning to the airport. A few seconds later, the plane crashed onto a golf course, killing three of the five family members on board.

I fly a variety of aircrafts about 200 hours per year. On multiple occasions, using a checklist has saved me from damaging the plane and probably injuring myself or others. Something as simple as latching a door can be the only difference in which side of the turf you reside.

The Brown M&M Caper

I have a confession to make: I'm a frustrated rock star. Save for my lack of any musical talent (I have lost friends after singing *Happy Birthday* to them), I could be Bruce Springsteen.

I once went to see Van Halen, a band fronted at that time by David Lee Roth. You may remember him. He was the alleged "nut-job" who insisted on having a large bowl of M&Ms provided to him backstage before concerts. He had one clause in his contract which required that no brown M&Ms were allowed in the bowl. If any brown M&Ms were found in the bowl, he had the unilateral right to cancel the show, with full compensation for the band.

As Roth explained in his book, *Crazy from the Heat*, Van Halen was one of the first groups to play in the large-scale stadium shows. They would arrive with ten large semi-trailer trucks full of equipment.

His contract read like the *Yellow Pages*. Deep in it, in Clause 126, was the "no brown M&M" sentence. Roth said if he saw one brown M&M in the bowl, he knew other items would be missed as well. On one occasion in Colorado, he found a single brown M&M and reportedly cancelled the sold-out concert.

Was this simply the result of a temper tantrum by a spoiled performer accustomed to always getting his way? By no means! In fact, it turned out that the promoter hadn't read the weight requirement for the stage, and the song *Jump* would have turned into *Fall*, as the entire staging would have plunged through the arena floor. Even "nut-job" David Lee Roth used a preconcert checklist. He was prepared!

Crazy? Overkill? Hell, no! On June 19, 2012, *USA Today* carried this report: "A drum technician was killed Saturday when a stage collapsed before a Radiohead concert in Toronto. . . the British man was in his mid-30s. He was trapped under the wreckage and pronounced dead at the scene. Investigators continued to sort through the rubble Sunday, trying to determine what caused the structure to come crashing down." One official described the stage as "fairly unstable," which strikes me as an understatement of epic proportions. Incidentally, the article also noted that all 40,000 tickets to the concert had been sold.

Tragically, this was not an isolated incident. There have been a series of concert stage collapses in recent years, including one in August 2011, when a concert stage in Indianapolis collapsed, killing six.

There's a centuries-old proverbial rhyme titled "For Want of a Nail," which goes like this:

> *For want of a nail, the shoe was lost.*
> *For want of a shoe, the horse was lost.*
> *For want of a horse, the rider was lost.*
> *For want of a rider, the message was lost.*
> *For want of a message, the battle was lost.*
> *For want of a battle, the kingdom was lost.*
> *And all for the want of a horseshoe nail.*

It might be time for a new version, to be called "For Want of a Brown M&M." I guess David Lee Roth isn't such a "nut job" after all.

Hero of the Hudson

Almost certainly, you're familiar with the story of an actual aircraft emergency which happened on January 15, 2009 and made headlines around the world. An early afternoon flight under the command of Captain Chesley "Sully" Sullenberger and it had just left New York's LaGuardia Airport bound for Charlotte, North Carolina when it experienced an emergency which put the lives of the crew and its 150 passengers in immediate and serious danger.

Climbing 3,000 feet with copilot Jeff Skiles flying the plane, U.S. Airways Flight 1549 crossed through a gaggle of geese, knocking out both engines.

The two aviators' training kicked in immediately. Though they had never flown together before, they were completely prepared to deal with the emergency, allowing them to proceed calmly and effectively. In *The Checklist Manifesto*, author Gawande described the scene: "There was no argument about what to do next, not even a discussion. And there was no need for one. The pilots' preparations had made them a team."

Sullenberger simply said, "My airplane" and took control. Skiles replied,: "Your aircraft," and went right for the checklist. First, he tried to relight both engines, then one engine. Investigators later commented that it was very remarkable that he was able to actually go through these procedures.

It quickly became apparent to both pilots that the crippled plane would be unable to return to LaGuardia or make it to any other nearby airports. Captain Sullenberger decided the only possible way to save his passengers and crew was to ditch the plane in the Hudson River. That he was able to so without any loss of life or serious injury made him an instant hero and the landing became known as "The Miracle on the Hudson."

"Sully" refused the hero's mantle. Amid the hoopla surrounding him in the days following the water landing, he said, "I want to correct the record right now. This was a crew effort." The outcome had as much to do with his skill as with teamwork and adherence to procedures and checklists. In other words, all the crew members, while they had never dealt with such an emergency, were nevertheless fully prepared to deal with it successfully.

Effort + Preparation = Excellence

Having illustrated what dangerous and tragic results can occur as a result of inadequate preparation and, inversely, the amazing results of the response to danger by a thoroughly trained and prepared flight crew, let me switch gears.

I began this chapter with some words of wisdom by a man named Joel Weldon.

You may not know who he is, so let me introduce you to him. A former construction worker, he turned down a four-year college scholarship because he thought he wasn't "smart enough" to go to college. For more than 37 years and counting, Joel has been one of the most highly respected and sought-after keynote speakers and sales trainers in North America, as well as an Idea Consultant and Executive Speech Coach for some of the world's foremost business leaders.

"At one time," he says, "I was so painfully shy that I couldn't even lead my Sunday school class in silent prayer." Yet, he was able to conquer his fears, becoming not just a much sought after speaker, but the only speaker to have earned all four of the highest honors in the speaking profession. For example, in 1989, Toastmasters International presented him with its highest award, the Golden Gavel, linking him with such notables as Walter Cronkite, Art Linkletter, Earl Nightingale, and Ken Blanchard.

With the approximately 3,000 speeches and seminars he has delivered during his career, one might suspect all Joel needs to do now when a new assignment comes along is to pack his bag and be on his way. But one would be wrong—very, very wrong. To this day, no matter how many times he's spoken to a particular group or on a particular subject, he spends 50 hours in preparation each and every time.

When asked why, he replies: "Because to be excellent, I know each idea must relate specifically to the audience. And excellence is the result of effort and preparation."

The Key Ingredient

While I don't know him personally and haven't heard him speak, I learned something about Joel Weldon that puts him in a special place in my personal Hall of Fame. While he may not typically face life-threatening emergencies in his profession, his use of checklists is as thorough and extensive as any I've ever encountered. That includes a travel checklist, a seminar set-up checklist, a presentation checklist, an after presentation checklist, and a facility checklist. Taken together, they cover about 700 items.

Listed items include his meeting materials, speaking materials, equipment, clothes, props, travel items, etc. There's virtually nothing that could happen from the time he leaves home until he returns that would find Joel unprepared. In his case, Murphy would have to rewrite his famous law to read: "Whatever can go wrong will go wrong, except where Joel Weldon's involved."

Have you ever attended a meeting where one of the speaker's handouts was a clothespin? If Joel had been the speaker, you probably have. It didn't take very many nights in hotel or motel rooms, lying awake because the drapes wouldn't close completely, for him to add that item to his travel checklist. Now, with the drapes blocking any light from disturbing him, he can count on a good night's sleep wherever he is—even when the wind blows.

———————————— **FOOD FOR THOUGHT** ————————————

- Checklists are a "slam dunk." Start using them today; you'll be amazed how much more you'll accomplish.

- Whether your preparation is more education, more mentors, more reading, or more checklists—when the time comes, you'll be thankful you were so well prepared.

IN OTHER WORDS

Little things make the difference. Everyone is well prepared in the big things, but only the winners perfect the little things.

~ Paul "Bear" Bryant

There is no shortcut to achievement. Life requires thorough preparation — veneer isn't worth anything.

~ George Washington Carver

Forewarned, forearmed; to be prepared is half the victory. Wisdom comes of such a recognition.

~ Miguel de Cervantes

By failing to prepare you are preparing to fail.

~ Benjamin Franklin

None of us suddenly becomes something overnight. The preparations have been in the making for a lifetime.

~ Gail Kathleen Godwin

We are all, it seems, saving ourselves for the Senior Prom. But many of us forget that somewhere along the way we must learn to dance.

~ Alan Harrington

The key is not the 'will to win' — everybody has that. It is the will to prepare to win that is important.

~ Bobby Knight

There is no road too long to the man who advances deliberately and without undue haste; there are no honors too distant to the man who prepares himself for them with patience.

~ Jean de La Bruyère

I will prepare and some day my chance will come.
~ Abraham Lincoln

In management, it's preparation, preparation, preparation.
But, be very, very careful. It's not the sheer magnitude of the
preparation that matters. It's the relevance of what you do.
Is it clear? Will it change behavior? Does it sizzle?
~ Harvey Mackay

Live neither in the past nor in the future, but let each day's
work absorb all your interest, energy and enthusiasm. The best
preparation for tomorrow is to do today's work superbly well.
~ Sir William Osler

By chance, you will say,
but chance only favors the mind which is prepared.
~ Louis Pasteur

Spectacular achievement is always preceded
by unspectacular preparation.
~ Robert H. Schuller

When opportunity comes, it's too late to prepare.
~ John Wooden

CHAPTER

Communication: A Lost Art

*The single biggest problem in communication
is the illusion that it has taken place.*
~ George Bernard Shaw

I must admit I'm not always the best or most appropriate in terms of my style or manner of communication. I've also learned over the years to take most things with a grain of salt (particularly if it's followed by a shot of tequila and a slice of lime), so I don't get too worked up over much of anything that's directed my way. This has been tested of late, but more on that later.

That said, I've learned a thing or two about how not to communicate and what not to say or write, mostly from experience. The following are styles of communication I frequently observe, which ultimately do little to further the intended discourse or outcome.

Non-verbal Communication

- Talking with your arms folded across your chest or with your fists clenched at your side. *(It conveys aggressiveness.)*

- Blowing your nose or wiping your mouth and then shaking someone's hand. *(I'm not sure what it conveys but it's disgusting.)*

- Rolling your eyes when someone is speaking to you. *(My children will tell you this is a sure way for me to say: "The last thing I want to do is hurt you, but it's still on the list.")*

- Talking over your shoulder while walking away or out of a room. *(It conveys disrespect.)*

- Crossing your legs and folding your arms while sitting. *(It conveys that you're hiding something, or that you're cold.)*

- Snapping gum or chewing with your mouth open. *(It conveys that your parents were first cousins.)*

- Shifting eyes or shifting back and forth while standing. *(It conveys that you're being deceitful or have to hit the bathroom!)*

- Staring at the opposite sex in an inappropriate manner while talking to them. *(Enough said, you know what I mean!)*

- Working, reading, texting, writing or watching TV while someone is trying to have a conversation with you. I'm guilty of this one and am still working on always being "present" in the moment. *(It conveys disrespect.)*

- Not making eye contact while speaking directly to others or shaking their hand while not looking at them. *(It conveys lack of confidence.)*

Written Communication

- Frequently misspelling words or writing in different tenses.

- Spelling someone's name incorrectly, despite it being part of the correct email address. *(This one always amazes me: "Dear Mr. Schoefelt," sent to jshufeldt@ingredientsofoutliers.com.)*

- Using excessive legalese in a document *(heretofore, etc.)*.

- Using email or written communication to convey important information that should be communicated in person. *(For example, telling a close friend or long-time business partner, via email or voice mail, that you'll be dissolving the relationship!)*

- CAPITALIZING EVERY WORD IN AN EMAIL OR TEXT MESSAGE.

- Using multiple exclamation points. *(I was sooooo drunk last night!!!!!!!!)*

- Using shortened versions of words or phrases in a business email. *(Examples: prolly, ur, OMG, IDK, lol, eieio.)*

- Multiple smiley faces, frowns or any other kind of word art in a business email.

- Creatively interchanging: to, too and two; your and you're; its and it's; and their, they're and there.

- Excessively long sentences without any punctuation really drive me crazy almost more so than anything else even chewing gum with an open mouth or swearing in a meeting or one time at band camp this guy like really thought he was cool and then started drinking OMG he was so drunk that his parents were called and then he like he passed out in front of me.

- Using "I" and "me" interchangeably. *("Him and me went to the tractor pull and drank Buds.")*

One caveat: grammar changes, rules change. What may be a no-no today is okay tomorrow. So don't be one who "doth protest too much, methinks!"

There's no question that we're turning into a nation of functional illiterates, so I was happy to learn that at least a few folks are trying to change it. Meet Jeff Deck, founder of the Typo Eradication Advancement League (TEAL). Jeff and his partner, Benjamin Herson, travel America "to stamp out as many typos as we can find, in public signage and other venues where innocent eyes may be befouled by vile stains on the delicate fabric of our language."

They visit stores, restaurants, and other facilities to fix typos, add missing apostrophes and delete incorrect ones on signs and billboards, often with permission of the owners and on occasion, without. Not surprisingly, one case in the latter category got them into a bit of trouble.

It happened at the Grand Canyon, operated by the National Park Service. Like most—perhaps all—government agencies, it isn't exactly known for either common sense or a sense of humor. It seems these desperadoes had corrected a couple of small signs, only to find themselves arrested and charged with "conspiracy to vandalize government property." They were sentenced to a year's probation and have been banned from national parks for a year.

Anyone seeing this pair perpetrating a similar crime is urged to call Silent Witness or the local police. Or just give them a well-deserved round of applause.

About the worst writing advice I've seen is to rely on spellcheck programs. A couple of years ago, a popular magazine published an article titled "How to Appear More Intelligent" and included this bit of really bad advice: "Spell-check. Seriously. This is one of the world's great inventions—maybe better than the wheel. Use it religiously to correct your typing mistakes."

Great invention? Better than the wheel? Not even close! Sure, a spellcheck program will catch some typing mistakes, but it will miss many others and its grammatical suggestions are generally wrong as well.

I have dozens of illustrations to prove my point, but I'll leave you with just one which, as a physician, really caught my eye. It was a magazine article in which the author described a hospital visit where a lab technician took "vile after vile of blood." What was especially vile was this bit of writing.

Verbal Communication

- Like saying "like" like every few words *(I, for one, don't like it.)*

- Using threats, "If you don't do XXX, then I'll do YYY!" *(The conversation can only go one direction from here. It's rarely positive, as you leave the recipient no way out.)*

- Speaking in the third person *(although this is really fun, saying "John's getting angry!" is like super annoying).*

- Mumbling, low-talking or talking into the hand *(sadly, I used to silently mouth words to my grandmother to see if I could make her tap her hearing aid. I'm sick, I know).*

- Saying "Whatever!" whenever something is annoying.

- When someone asks a legitimate question, respond by exclaiming, "I can't believe you didn't know that!" *(Conveys that you believe the person's that stupid.)*

- Saying "Trust me," and then proceeding to say something completely untrue.

- Trailing off in midsentence and waiting for someone else to finish your sentence. "In 1930, the Republican controlled House of Representatives, in an effort to alleviate the effects of the... anyone, anyone, Great Depression, passed the... anyone, anyone, tariff bill, the Hawley Smoot tariff act which ... anyone, anyone, raised or lowered... anyone, anyone, Buehler?"

- Interrupting while the other person is still speaking.

Perhaps the worst "crime" in this category, one that has taken on epic proportions, is the dreadfully annoying "ya' know." And it's by no means limited to the poorly educated members of our society. For example, professional actress and television personality Whoopi Goldberg, when she was a guest on the Fox New program *Hannity*, used the expression numerous times.

Well-educated Caroline Kennedy, daughter of the late JFK, used it many times a few years ago in attempting to explain why, ya' know, she thought she should, ya' know, be given Hillary Clinton's seat in the

U.S. Senate. The ridicule heaped on her as a result may have had something to do with why, ya' know, she eventually withdrew.

Dropping the Ball

So far in this chapter, most of what we've written deals with just one side of the communication process. The reason for what George Bernard Shaw called, "the illusion that it has taken place" is because most of what's defined as communication is really one-directional activity, with no awareness of what's missing. The individual who's speaking or writing isn't communicating until and unless there's a recipient to whom he or she is speaking or writing. The missing link in the communication process is the listener.

The late Mortimer Adler, a popular American author and educator, described that process well. "Communication," he said, "is like playing catch. Catching is as much of a skill as throwing, though it is a skill of a different kind." Unfortunately, instead of catching what's been thrown, we seem to keep dropping the ball, and we've been doing so for a long time.

Long before David Letterman or Jay Leno appeared on the scene, Steve Allen was the king of late-night television. As a regular feature on *The Tonight Show*, Allen would leave the stage and walk down among the audience. Stopping at one row, he'd whisper a brief statement to the person in the aisle seat, who was to quietly repeat it to the person in the adjacent seat, and so on until it reached the far end of that aisle.

Allen would then have that last person repeat the statement aloud while at the same time the original statement would appear on the screen. Invariably, there was little or no resemblance between the two, resulting in gales of laughter from the audience. Nevertheless, it clearly demonstrated that we're a nation of non-listeners—and that was more than a half-century ago.

Ever since, that sorry fact has been noted again and again. In 1982, newspaper columnist Jim Sanderson called listening: "one of the great lost arts in human relationships. People instinctively react to any opening you give them to talk about themselves." A few years later (1988), well-known author and speaker Leo F. Buscaglia commented: "It seems that few people listen anymore... I'm beginning to wonder if they [listeners] are a vanishing breed."

The Listening Stick

One man was so convinced that listening had become a lost art that he decided to mount a campaign to restore it. His name was Ben John Joyce, a California-based consultant and entrepreneur, and the founder of The Center for Applied Excellence. Its Mission Statement: "We teach people how to communicate."

His stated position on listening got right to the point. "Listening," he said, "is a skill that has a dreadfully limited number of truly effective practitioners. We're not taught to listen in school, at home, or at work. On the contrary, we learn the communications process from authority figures whose specialty seems to be talking."

While I had never heard of Joyce, a colleague of mine, Bob Kelly, knew him well and has copies of Joyce's listening campaign materials in his files. The centerpiece is a small wooden stick, about the size of a tongue depressor, and appropriately named "The Listening Stick." Printed on one side are these words: "Please, will you listen to me?" The reverse side has just two words: "Thank you."

Simple and straightforward, but Ben wasn't leaving anything to chance. The Listening Stick system included two other pieces: a Quick Use Guide and an Owner's Manual. The former is the size of a business card with a foldout feature containing bullet points on listening well.

The Owner's Manual goes into greater detail on what it takes to become a good listener and how to handle situations when the person to whom you're speaking appears not to be listening. It includes four types of behavior that interfere with the listener's ability to comprehend your message:

1. The listener has the attention span of a flashbulb.
2. The listener listens with a stop watch.
3. The listener becomes the speaker.
4. The speaker, sensing that the listener is not listening, raises the decibel level.

When any or all of these conditions occur, the Owner's Manual offers this advice:

"When you discover you are talking to someone who is not listening, stop talking. You have no obligation to provide background noise as accompaniment to whatever distracting activity that currently holds their interest. Neither is it helpful for you to enter into a competition for their attention by talking louder. The other person will have even less concern for listening to you and might even get annoyed if you raise the decibel level.

Simply stop talking and sit quietly. Almost everyone will listen long enough to learn why you fell silent. You will find in many cases that you have created an attentive, if somewhat sheepish, listener. Don't be concerned. The sheepishness will pass quickly. Be sure to thank those who listen effectively.

Help those who persist in not listening to you by handing them the Listening Stick, question side up. Explain to those who agree to listen that you would like them to hold the Listening Stick to signify that they are listening. At any point, they can indicate that they are through listening by putting it down."

I'm sorry I never got to know Ben Joyce and that his death in 1996 put an end to his campaign. I can recall many occasions when I'd have found the Listening Stick a very handy device and I suspect that many of my family members, friends, clients, patients, colleagues and others with whom I've communicated over the years might well have wished for a similar tool to hand me or to hit me with on occasion.

As the noise at every level of our society keeps getting louder and louder, it's important for us to keep in mind that communication is a two-way street. Completing the circuit requires patience, understanding, and civility by all who wish to participate effectively in the—ya' know—communication process!

FOOD FOR THOUGHT

- My goal is to be more "present" during conversations—no texting, emailing, or interrupting. What's yours?

- One of my earlier role models in residency was a 3rd year resident named Judy. What I remember most about her was her ability to focus completely on the person with whom she was interacting. It could be a drunken patient or a screaming gang member, but no matter who they were, they felt they had her undivided attention.

IN OTHER WORDS

Instead of talking in the hope that people will listen,
try listening to people in the hope that they will talk.
~ Mardy Grothe

The two words 'information' and 'communication' are often
used interchangeably, but they signify quite different things.
Information is giving out; communication is getting through.
~ Sydney J. Harris

Be different – if you don't have the facts and knowledge
required, simply listen. When word gets out that you can listen
when others tend to talk, you will be treated as a sage.
~ Edward Koch

*Agree to these ground rules: Be curious, conversational and
real. Don't persuade or interrupt. Listen, listen, listen.*
~ Elizabeth Lesser

*Good communication is as stimulating as black coffee,
and just as hard to sleep after.*
~ Anne Morrow Lindbergh

*Listening well is as powerful a means of communication
and influence as to talk well.*
~ John Marshall

*Years ago, I tried to top everybody, but I don't anymore.
I realized it was killing conversation.
When you're always trying for a topper
you aren't really listening. It ruins communication.*
~ Groucho Marx

*The marvels – of film, radio, and television – are marvels of
one-way communication, which is not communication at all.*
~ Milton Mayer

*Listening is a magnetic and strange thing, a creative force.
The friends who listen to us are the ones we move toward.
When we are listened to, it creates us,
makes us unfold and expand.*
~ Karl Menninger

*The art of effective listening is essential
to clear communication, and clear communication
is necessary to management success.*
~ J.C. Penney

*The more we elaborate our means of communication,
the less we communicate.*
~ J. B. Priestley

Communication is at the heart of everything we do.
It is the foundation for interaction among human beings.
~ Nido R. Qubein

Most men talk at one another rather than with one another.
Each person thinks he is making meaningful points, but rarely
do they add up to genuine communication.
~ Eugene Rand

CHAPTER

Imperturbability: Staying Calm

Thou must be like a promontory of the sea,
against which, though the waves beat continually,
yet it both itself stands, and about it are
those swelling waves stilled and quieted.

~ Marcus Aurelius

In this age of technology and instant everything, which arrived with visions and promises of greater efficiency and effectiveness, we were assured that by now we'd be enjoying lives of greater leisure and pleasure than ever before. Instead, stress levels are sky-high as we collectively bemoan the gloom and doom that awaits our children and grandchildren. Do you know anyone who hasn't stated, "Oh, my Gosh, I am so stressed!"? It seems as though Uncle Sam, the once tall and proud symbol of our nation, has been replaced by Chicken Little, of "The Sky Is Falling" fame.

In that 19th century fable, you may recall the main character is bopped on the head by a falling acorn. Immediately concluding that the entire sky is falling, he rallies his animal friends and they dash off to alert the king of the impending doom. In the end, their fate varies, for better or worse, depending on which of the many versions you read.

I believe there are better lessons we can learn from the past than the imminent collapse of the sky. I have two stories to tell you, both of which involve men born back in Chicken Little's day, but of flesh and blood, not fantasy or fable.

One, who would become a world-renowned physician, was born in Canada in 1849. The other, born in 1865 to an English couple living in India, became famous as a Nobel Prize-winning short-story writer and poet.

The Physician

In 1872, William Osler received his medical degree from McGill University in Montreal. After postgraduate studies abroad, he returned to Canada in 1874 and joined the McGill faculty. In 1884, he left to become professor of clinical medicine at the University of Pennsylvania. Known for his innovative approach to treating patients, his reputation grew rapidly and, in 1888, he was recruited to become physician-in-chief of the soon to be opened Johns Hopkins Hospital in Baltimore and as professor of medicine of its planned school of medicine. To this day, Osler is recognized as one of the fathers of modern medicine.

As he prepared to leave the University of Pennsylvania for his new assignment, Osler gave a farewell address to his medical students. Titled, "Aequanimitas," it has become famous for its enduring wisdom and practicality. The Latin word, defined by Osler as imperturbability, is emblazoned on the Johns Hopkins School of Medicine shield and every incoming intern is given a copy of Osler's message. While addressed specifically to those in medicine, the following excerpts illustrate its application in virtually every field of endeavor.

> *In the first place, in the physician or surgeon no quality takes rank with imperturbability, and I propose for a few minutes to direct your attention to this essential bodily virtue. Perhaps I may be able to give those of you, if it has not developed during the critical scenes of the past month, a hint or two of its importance,*

possibly a suggestion for its attainment. Imperturbability means coolness and presence of mind under all circumstances, calmness amid storm, clearness of judgment in moments of grave peril, immobility, impassiveness…

Replace the words "physician or surgeon" with "entrepreneur, small-business owner, attorney, pilot, athlete, entertainer, homemaker, manager, human," or whatever title best describes you and I can say with confidence that, based on my own experience, the message is as pertinent today as it was 120-plus years ago.

During the years I've spent in hospital emergency departments and in managing urgent care centers, I've witnessed the occasional provider, and more than a few operators, become unhinged during real or imagined crises. Nothing does more to raise the anxiety of patients or employees than to see the person upon whose expertise they're relying on, "lose it."

Despite its clear necessity, I'm uncertain if calmness under pressure comes from genes or training. Osler had this to say:

As imperturbability is largely a bodily endowment, I regret to say that there are those amongst you, who, owing to congenital defects, may never be able to acquire it. Education, however, will do much; and, with practice and experience, the majority of you may expect to attain to a fair measure. The first essential is to have your nerves well in hand.

How then does one become the face of serenity during the storm? Clearly, training and experience count for much; I can remember my hand trembling the first time I sutured a patient or delivered a baby. I like to think that, after the first few seconds, I regained my steadiness and that the patient's laceration eventually healed and the child was born without shaken baby syndrome.

Congenital defects aside, Doctor Osler also recognized the possibility of disappointment and failure:

It is sad to think that, for some of you, there is in store disappointment, perhaps failure. You cannot hope, of course, to escape from the cares and anxieties incident to professional life. Stand up bravely, even against the worst. Remember, too, that sometimes "from our desolation only does the better life begin." Even with disaster ahead and ruin imminent, it is better to face them with a smile and with the head erect than to crouch at their approach. It has been said that, "in patience ye, shall win your souls," and what is this patience but an equanimity which enables you to rise superior to the trials of life.

For anyone who has started a venture that ultimately failed, as I have, or for those who've struggled but have eventually succeeded, take some comfort in that ultimately you're better for the effort—success or failure.

The Poet

The second nineteenth century figure I referred to earlier was Rudyard Kipling, whose poems have long been staples in English literature classes. They include "Mandalay" and "Gunga Din," both based on military life in British-colonial India, where Kipling grew up. The latter poem, which ends with these famous words: "You're a better man than I am, Gunga Din," was twice the subject of Hollywood films.

Released in 1939, the first one featured such well-known film stars of the day as Cary Grant and Joan Fontaine. In typical Hollywood fashion, a second version was released in 1961, with numerous changes. Featuring Frank Sinatra and his famous (or infamous) Rat Pack, it was renamed *Sergeants 3* and was reset in the Old West with the role of the native water-carrier Gunga Din played by none other than Sammy Davis, Jr.

But I digress. It was another Kipling poem, written at close to the same time as *Aequanimitas*, that expressed much the same underlying message, but in simpler terms. Unlike Osler's twelve-letter title, Kipling's poem was simply titled *if.* Rather than repeat the entire thirty-two-line poem here, the following are some excerpts:

If you can keep your head when all about you
Are losing theirs and blaming it on you,
If you can trust yourself when all men doubt you,
But make allowance for their doubting too . . .

If you can dream – and not make dreams your master;
If you can think – and not make thoughts your aim;
If you can meet with Triumph and Disaster
And treat those two impostors just the same . . .

If you can force your heart and nerve and sinew
To serve your turn long after they are gone,
And so hold on when there is nothing in you
Except the Will which says to them: 'Hold on!' . . .

If you can fill the unforgiving minute
With sixty seconds' worth of distance run,
Yours is the Earth and everything that's in it,
And – which is more – you'll be a Man, my son!

The words of Osler and Kipling don't deny the possibility of a falling sky, nor do they recommend a "pie in the sky/by and by" kind of mentality. Their words are about attitude, about maintaining a calm and even-tempered outlook, regardless of circumstances.

We may not encounter the word "equanimity" very often, but consider these definitions:

- A habit of mind that is only rarely disturbed
- Evenness of mind under stress
- A calmness of mind under all circumstances

A Tremendous Example

One man who perhaps best exemplified this kind of attitude was the late Charlie "Tremendous" Jones, who from 1965 until his death in 2008, traveled the world as a professional speaker and humorist. During his career, he received virtually every honor in the speaking profession, and was ranked by his peers as one of the top fifty speakers of the twentieth century.

Despite a series of health issues, including the prostate cancer that would eventually claim his life, Jones continued to spread his wise and humor-filled message in a manner unlike anyone else. Despite his own always positive and upbeat approach to life, he would proclaim to his audiences: "Show me a positive thinker, and I'll show you an idiot." As the laughter would subside, he'd explain that the key didn't lie in being a positive thinker, but a positive *realist*! "Sure you have problems," he'd say. "You're not dead—and they're going to get WORSE!"

It wasn't a lack of empathy or compassion on his part that triggered such statements. He'd then proceed to tell his audiences that he'd discovered the greatest secret in the world. After a lengthy buildup, he'd pause dramatically for a minute or two, ask the audience if they were ready and would announce: "Here it comes, the greatest secret in the world," and then bellow: "NOTHING WORKS!"

Jones wanted people to recognize that things will go wrong, that there will be problems all through life, but if we learn to accept that fact, maybe we'll begin to take ourselves less seriously. "You have two choices," he'd explain. "When facing the problems you'll encounter, you can choose to be 'miserable miserable' or 'happy miserable.'"

Charlie "Tremendous" Jones' advice was the same as that offered by Sir William Osler and Rudyard Kipling a century earlier, as well as that of Marcus Aurelius, a Roman emperor of two millennia ago, whose words introduced this chapter. Yet I find it fascinating that we still occasionally have to be reminded of the wisdom of this advice. Imperturbability (or aequanimitas), whether acquired or developed, is an incredibly beneficial trait which will make the transit through this life much more enjoyable.

Or in simpler terms, as Judge Elihu Smails said in the film *Caddyshack*: "It's easy to grin when your ship comes in, and you've got the stock market beat. But the man worthwhile is the man who can smile, when his shorts are too tight in the seat."

──────── FOOD FOR THOUGHT ────────

- Losing your cool never furthers your cause. Yelling, swearing, screaming, etc. always pushes you and others farther away from your desired outcome.

- When everything else is out of control, at the very least, you can control your own reactions.

- Stress reveals character.

──────── IN OTHER WORDS ────────

The spirit of man should be like a lake unruffled by wind or storm.

~ Annie Besant

The pursuit, even of the best things, ought to be calm and tranquil.

~ Marcus Tullius Cicero

Maintain composure in times of heightened emotion, reacting only when thoughts are calm and clear. Being sensible will open doors for solutions and creativity.

~ Jaren L. Davis

Nothing gives one person so much advantage over another as to remain always cool and unruffled under all circumstances.

~ Thomas Jefferson

He who has faith has... an inward reservoir of
courage, hope, confidence, calmness, and assuring trust
that all will come out well - even though to the world
it may appear to come out most badly.
~ B.C. Forbes

Do everything quietly and in a calm spirit.
Do not lose your inner peace for anything whatsoever,
even if your whole world seems upset.
~ Saint Francis de Sales

My father used to say to me, "Whenever you get into a jam,
whenever you get into a crisis or an emergency,
become the calmest person in the room
and you'll be able to figure your way out of it.
~ Rudolph Giuliani

Calmness is the cradle of power.
~ Josiah Gilbert Holland

When we are unable to find tranquility within ourselves,
it is useless to seek it elsewhere.
~ François de La Rochefoucauld

Thinking is, or ought to be, a coolness and a calmness; and our
poor hearts throb, and our poor brains beat too much for that.
~ Herman Melville

The cyclone derives its powers from a calm center.
So does a person.
~ Norman Vincent Peale

Happy is the man who can endure the highest and the lowest
fortune. He who has endured such vicissitudes with
equanimity has deprived misfortune of its power.
~ Seneca

Great people are not affected by each puff of wind
that blows ill. Like great ships, they sail serenely on,
in a calm sea or a great tempest.

~ George Washington

CHAPTER

Tolerating Risk: Being a Doer, not a Dreamer

A lot of people have ideas, but there are few who
decide to do something about them now. Not tomorrow.
Not next week. But today.
The true entrepreneur is a doer, not a dreamer.

~ Nolan Bushnell

Years ago, in the Funky Winkerbean comic strip, Tony, the owner of the local pizza joint, is giving some business advice to the teenaged Funky and his friends. I don't remember the exact words, but Tony explains to them that the way to make a small fortune in business is—to start out with a large fortune. By the way, the same holds true in aviation. The standing joke is that if you want to make a lot of money in aviation, start with a lot of money. Just ask Frank Lorenzo, former CEO of bankrupt Eastern Airlines.

Sure it's an old gag and it was meant for laughs, but business history is filled with stories of would-be entrepreneurs who learned the hard way that there was nothing funny about it. In some circles, reports of failure after failure have given entrepreneurism a bad name.

Throughout history, entrepreneurs have faced harsh critics. From Shakespeare's *The Merchant of Venice* through Oliver Stone's movie *Wall Street* ("Greed is good, greed works," etc.) entrepreneurial efforts are cast in a dim light. Often the budding entrepreneur has only himself or herself to blame, having fallen so much in love with that "Big Idea," that reality has flown out the window. (I can relate; stay tuned.)

To paraphrase, Lifebook founder Jon Butcher said, "No other social system can compete with the free-market, entrepreneurial system in terms of productivity, raising living standards, and creating prosperity... Yet, despite its overwhelming contributions, some elements of society still associate profit-making with vice."

When it comes to entrepreneurial ventures, I'm all in favor of developing a positive attitude, as long as there's some common sense mixed in with it. Norman Vincent Peale's advice that, "It's always too early to quit," works fine as a life motto, but doesn't necessarily apply to every situation we face. The same is true for the famous statement from nineteenth century British writer William E. Hickson: "If at first you don't succeed, try, try again."

Again, that's okay up to a point. But to cite another old truism, there can come a time to "stop beating a dead horse." W.C. Fields, the legendary actor, comedian, writer, and curmudgeon of the early twentieth century put it this way: "If at first you don't succeed, try, try again. Then quit. There's no use being a damn fool about it."

As you'll see shortly, I've found myself astride dead horses on occasion but, fortunately, I'd been made aware of the tribal wisdom of the Dakota Indians. Passed down from generation to generation, it states simply: "When you discover you're riding a dead horse, the best strategy is to dismount." Accordingly, when I've faced such conditions, I've usually been able to get out of the saddle before too much damage, financial or otherwise, has been done—keyword, *usually*.

Failure to follow that advice can, and likely will, have serious consequences. Desperate business owners and managers, refusing to recognize the horse's demise, have been known to try various "solutions," including these, which have been floating around on the Internet for quite some time:

- Buying stronger whips

- Changing riders

- Threatening the horse with termination

- Appointing a committee to study the horse

- Arranging to visit other sites to see how they ride dead horses

- Lowering the standards so dead horses can be included

- Reclassifying the dead horse as "living-impaired"

- Changing the form to read: "This horse is not dead"

- Hiring outside contractors to ride the dead horse

- Harnessing several dead horses together for increased speed

- Donating the dead horse to a recognized charity, thereby deducting its full original cost

- Providing additional funding to increase the dead horse's performance

- Doing a time management study to see if lighter riders would improve productivity

- Declaring a dead horse has lower overhead and therefore performs better

- Forming a focus group to identify profitable uses for dead horses

- Rewriting the performance requirements for all horses

- Promoting the dead horse to a supervisory position.

A Horse of My Own

Among the horses that died on me while I was galloping merrily along was one I'd named Vibrapon. It was a product I'd designed for women and it employed low-level vibrations to increase blood flow to muscle tissue, thereby relieving menstrual cramps caused by uterine contractions and lower blood flow to the uterus. I figured if a tampon could incorporate this small, non-disposable, removable component, it would be a huge hit! I even had the first commercial written. "I used to hate that time of the month until I discovered the Vibrapon. Now I almost look forward to getting my period."

Unfortunately, I learned that someone had already (uhh) conceived and patented the Vibrapon, though the fact that no one has ever heard of it probably doesn't speak well for its success. Lesson: You have to be a risk taker to start a business and have the vision to see it through.

This also bears out an important tip: check the U.S. Patent and Trademark Office website (*www.uspto.gov*) before spending any capital on what you believe to be an innovative idea. Ob-Gyn friends have told my why, physiologically speaking, the Vibrapon was doomed for failure—it has to do with prostaglandins and other pain causing chemicals. Despite this, I had no shortage of woman volunteers wanting to try the beta version.

Pressing On

To me, entrepreneurism is simply taking something you're passionate about and turning it into capital so you can do more of it. Passion without monetization is called a hobby.

I'm what you'd call a serial entrepreneur; I've tried (and more often than not, failed) at more businesses than you can imagine. (You may recall my hot dog stand adventure and others that I described in Chapter 2.) Although failing's never fun, if you keep your mind open it will teach you more than success ever will. So let's look at and discuss some characteristics of successful entrepreneurs and share a story or two about those traits.

Visionary/Risk-taking

Being visionary can be both a blessing and a curse. Decide if you are an innovator, early adopter, or superior operator.

Innovation can be a risky business inasmuch as you end up telling the masses that they're in need of something of which they're currently unaware.

Being an early adopter has some benefits. You let the innovator pave the way by educating the masses and hitting all the landmines.

A superior operator is something all entrepreneurs have to become to achieve any lasting success.

I began this chapter with a quote by Nolan Bushnell. You may not recognize that name, so let me tell you a little about him. Born in 1943, he went on to earn a degree in electrical engineering. But it was while working at an amusement park during his high school and college years that his vision began to take shape; it was the midway arcade games that drew most of his attention.

During his career, Bushnell has started more than 20 companies, primarily in the game industry. They include such well-known names as Atari, Inc. and Chuck E. Cheese's Pizza-Time Theaters. He's been inducted into the Video Game Hall of Fame and was named by *Newsweek* magazine as one of the "50 Men Who Changed America." His definition of a true entrepreneur as "a doer, not a dreamer" fits him well.

Another serial entrepreneur, 20 years younger than Bushnell, is Warren Struhl. He currently holds the position of Chief Inspiration Officer at Successories, Inc., the leading inspirational, motivational, and recognition products company he acquired in 2008. Years earlier, at age 25, he founded his first business, PaperDirect, Inc. Five years later, with more than $100 million in sales, he sold the business to a Fortune 500 company.

That began a series of launching a dozen or more ventures in rapid succession. In addition to his Successories post, he partnered with famous basketball star LeBron James and others to co-found Purebrands, LLC, producer of the popular SHEETS Energy Strips.

Struhl is also a published author; his book, *Starting Them UP*, released in 2010, is subtitled: *Timely, Under-the-Hood Insights for Entrepreneurs by a Serial Starter and a Bunch of His Entrepreneurial Friends*. In the opening chapter he writes: "Possessing the 'DNA' of an entrepreneur means being a fearless, fiercely motivated self-starter."

Then he adds these cautionary words: "The roller-coaster, often rough-and-tumble high-stakes world of the start-up entrepreneur may not be an ideal career choice for the faint of heart or the risk-averse."

Personally, I can't really think of anything worth achieving that's not high risk. It may not be life threatening and you may not lose a lot of money, but there is risk involved. Changing jobs, moving, and venturing out of your comfort zone are all risky endeavors. Some of the coolest sports I know are the most risky—hang gliding, scuba diving, and base jumping. Some people believe the rewards are absolutely worthwhile. That's not to recommend you go out and do extreme sports or anything else. It's simply that great rewards are often the result of calculated risks.

The good news is that I've made every mistake in the business play-book—some of them nearly fatal. In the end, it will work out, no one is dying, and chances are I'll be better off.

If you invest in a start-up company the risks are very high; most of them fail miserably. However if it works, the upside may be worth the risk. If not, when it all blows up and you look and feel like a fool, be secure enough to laugh at yourself.

Integrity/Detail-oriented

Setting the integrity bar high (more on that later) is a must for the successful entrepreneur. At one point in our history, I had someone working for me who was the embodiment of hard work. She worked night and day and knew every aspect of the business. She just had two little issues.

The first was that she was like Chicken Little—the sky in her world was always falling, though she was always there to save the day. I learned over time that she devised some of these tragedies so she could come to the rescue and prove her value. This annoying trait was tolerable, at least for the short-term.

The other trait, embezzling, was the elephant in the room. She would enter one thing in the financial software and then manually make the check out to her husband's

business. I eventually caught on. The problem was that I was working day and night trying to maintain cash flow and took my eye off the books. Ergo, I was not detail-oriented. Such lack of attention, particularly during the start-up phase, can be disastrous.

Ambitious/Motivated

Pardon the vernacular, but if you want to be an entrepreneur, you have to *get your ass out of the chair* and roll up your sleeves. Or, as I mentioned to one of our emergency department nurses who happened to be sitting in a chair for quite a while as the department sunk into chaos, "I'm not sure if you've heard of Newton, but I can assure you, gravity will keep the chair from flying away if you get your rear end out of it."

Anyone can talk the game. Succeeding takes someone who is motivated to not just start a business, but to see it through. "You have to be wired a certain way to be an entrepreneur," Struhl says. "You have to be obsessive. If you're not thinking about it 24/7, you're probably not entrepreneurial material." Remember the old adage: if this was easy, everyone would do it.

One caveat: all the ambition in the world won't save a bad idea. Or as the fake Successories poster says, "When you earnestly believe you can compensate for a lack of skill by doubling your efforts, there's no end to what you can't do!"

Optimistic/Adaptable

I'm optimistic, probably to a fault. This optimism allows me to approach challenges in a way that helps me look at them as opportunities as opposed to obstacles. However, I don't mean you should be a Pollyanna. You should be approaching challenges with the requisite diligence and concern. Despite this, you can always find a silver lining in almost every situation.

Here's why I'm optimistic. I've learned from experience that things generally work out. I also know I usually end up in a better place after they do. I always learn something and I like a challenge. Part of this is from my emergency medicine background. It goes back to this thought: no one is dying, so how bad could it be?

Note: there *is* a downside to perpetual blind optimism, though. It happens when you fail to recognize the danger from a large impediment or barrier because you're so busy discounting its importance and looking for the silver lining.

I work with a fantastic team of realists who have the ability to see both sides of the issue and who will occasionally focus on the negative side. I'm sure there are times when my always-optimistic outlook drives them crazy. I know for a fact that attitude has driven at least one CFO to insanity (though I think he may have already been part way around the bend when he came on board—he had a riding crop mounted on the wall in the office).

Anyway, at one point of my business life we were trying to grow the business with very little capital. In 1995 I had the brilliant (not really) idea to franchise the concept. After two years, I thought we had a pretty good operating model that could be reproducible in other markets.

In essence, we adapted to our lack of capitalization by selling our platform. We learned, however, that providing healthcare isn't a model that's easily franchiseable, mainly because there's no way to protect your brand. One bad apple could destroy the entire entity by providing less than acceptable service or care.

While we were slugging it out trying to promote this concept, someone from the *Wall Street Journal* left a message for me to call him as soon as possible. I thought we were finally going to get some recognition for this—at the time,—ground-breaking idea. After three days of phone tag, I finally reached him. "Dr. Shufeldt, it's great to finally get to speak with you. Would you like to increase your subscription from one year to two?"

Nevertheless, I remain optimistic.

Postscript: As luck would have it, I had the opportunity to again franchise urgent care centers. Not learning from my first foray, I had to learn the hard lesson again. This time, not only was it some of the franchisees with a small taste of success who "knew it all," it was two of my "partners" who agreed with them. Time will tell but for, my money, I'm betting on red (ink).

Sense of Humor/Humility

Another essential quality the successful entrepreneur must have is a sense of humor. Things will go wrong, often at the most unexpected and inopportune times. The customer who came to my hot dog stand and announced to all within earshot that I was the doctor who'd treated him in the emergency department a week earlier is a case in point. An embarrassing moment? You bet it was! But I still laugh every time I think about it.

A sense of humor is what keeps an entrepreneur sane. Failing to see the humor in all the crazy things you'll experience will make the ride much less enjoyable.

In healthcare, a lack of sense of humor can be your undoing. I can't tell you how many times I've looked around an exam room for the Candid Camera film crew, believing that the only explanation for what a patient just said was that I must be getting "punked." *("Wait, you were standing on a bridge huffing paint and then you fell off the bridge and only broke your ankle, and then stood up and were struck by a truck?")*

Ethel Barrymore, legendary actress of the early twentieth century, once commented: "You grow up the day you have the first real laugh—at yourself." And the late inspirational writer and poet William Arthur Ward expressed that same idea: "To be able to laugh at yourself is maturity."

To be able to laugh at oneself not only demonstrates maturity but also humility. The proud and the arrogant can never laugh off a mistake or an embarrassment. It would be an admission that they aren't quite as perfect as they'd like people to believe.

The challenge with arrogance is twofold. Everyone loves to see arrogant people fail and will often go out of their way to *not* help an arrogant person. Arrogant people are usually deeply insecure and, as such, will never take a risk that could result in them being viewed as failures. The most competent people I know are also the most humble.

The goal of any entrepreneur is to make a contribution and to be paid a fair price at some time for the business. However, the most important advice I can offer is this:

While the payout is great, the fun is in the ride, not arriving at the destination. Or as Steve Jobs remarked, "The reward is the journey."

———————— FOOD FOR THOUGHT ————————

- Here's the "takeaway" message: Most things work out; if they don't—I hope you'll learn something, perhaps get a good story out of it, and, possibly, never make the mistake again. So, what's not to like?

- If you want to grow, you have to risk.

IN OTHER WORDS

*Entrepreneurs average 3.8 failures before final success. What
sets the successful ones apart is their amazing persistence.*

~ Lisa M. Amos

*The entrepreneur always searches for change, responds to it,
and exploits it as an opportunity.*

~ Peter F. Drucker

*The entrepreneur in us sees opportunities everywhere we look,
but many people see only problems everywhere they look.
The entrepreneur in us is more concerned with
discriminating between opportunities than he or she is
with failing to see the opportunities.*

~ Michael Gerber

*I'm convinced that about half of what separates the successful
entrepreneurs from the non-successful ones is pure perseverance.*

~ Steve Jobs

*Entrepreneurs are risk takers, willing to roll the dice with
their money or reputation on the line in support of an idea or
enterprise. They willingly assume responsibility for the success
or failure of a venture and are answerable for all its facets.*

~ Victor Kiam

*Going into business for yourself, becoming an entrepreneur,
is the modern-day equivalent of pioneering on the old frontier.*

~ Paula Nelson

*The cover-your-butt mentality of the workplace will get you
only so far. The follow-your-gut mentality of the entrepreneur
has the potential to take you anywhere you want to go.*

~ Bill Rancic

Entrepreneurs and their small enterprises are responsible for almost all the economic growth in the United States.
~ Ronald Reagan

Emphasize a strong commitment to reinvention and self-renewal to keep the entrepreneurial spirit alive. It encourages innovation.
~ Howard Schulz

Entrepreneurs have to figure out how to morph themselves into something better. You can't sit on your laurels on any component of your business life.
~ Charles Schwab

The entrepreneur is essentially a visualizer and an actualizer. He can visualize something, and when he visualizes it, he sees exactly how to make it happen.
~ Robert L. Schwartz

Entrepreneurs are risk takers, willing to roll the dice with their money or reputations on the line in support of an idea or enterprise.
~ Victoria Claflin Woodhull

CHAPTER

Kindness: The Art of Paying It Forward

*Perhaps you will forget tomorrow the kind words you say
today, but the recipient may cherish them over a lifetime.*

~ Dale Carnegie

The famous French author and aviator Antoine de Saint-Exupéry was
born into an aristocratic family in 1900. Growing up, he wasn't a particularly good student, and at age 21 he entered military service with
the French Army. After taking private flying lessons, he accepted a
transfer to the French Air Force. Back in civilian life in 1926, he
resumed flying and became one of the pioneers in flying international
mail routes, a dangerous job in those early days of aviation.

At about that same time, Saint-Exupéry began to write and would
often record his thoughts while flying his plane. His first book was
published in 1929 and he was soon recognized as a rising star in literary
circles. His writing success, however, in no way diminished his love
affair with flying.

While competing in an air race in 1935, his plane crashed in the Sahara
Desert. He and his navigator wandered for four days and were close to
death when they were found and rescued. Four years later, his semi-
autobiographical book, *Wind, Sand and Stars*, told the story of that

close encounter, along with other reflections. It won the U.S. National Book Award, further establishing his reputation as an author.

Among those reflections is a vivid passage that describes an experience he had while riding on a commuter bus and listening to the conversations of some of the homeward-bound "worn out clerks" sitting near him. Saint-Exupéry wrote:

> *"I heard them talking to one another in murmurs and whispers. They talked about illness, money, shabby domestic cares. Their talk painted the walls of the dismal prison in which these men had locked themselves up. And suddenly, I had a vision of the face of destiny.*
>
> *Old bureaucrat, my comrade, it is not you who are to blame. No one ever helped you to escape.... . Nobody grasped you by the shoulder while there was still time. Now the clay of which you were shaped has dried and hardened, and naught in you will ever awaken the sleeping musician, the poet, the astronomer that possibly inhabited you in the beginning."*

What a sad and dreary picture. Imagine what a difference a bit of kindness might have made in the lives of those men, had someone grasped them by the shoulder "while there was still time," before the clay of which they were shaped had dried and hardened. Simply showing them they mattered, that someone cared, might well have awakened them, allowing them to reach heights beyond their wildest dreams.

A Touch on the Shoulder

But we can do more than imagine it. Consider the story of Dudley Henrique who was—literally—touched on the shoulder by a stranger, a kind touch that would mark the beginning of a new life, while there was still time.

Dudley's early life wasn't easy. Born in 1937, he was six when his parents divorced. His mother was soon remarried—to a hot-tempered man who would beat him severely and often. Two years later his grandmother came to his rescue, taking him to live with her in Wilmington, Delaware. He never saw his mother again.

He spent the next eight years living with his grandmother, a working woman who had little time for him. Not surprisingly, he often got into trouble and, at 15, was expelled from school. His grandmother then enrolled him in a military academy known for working with problem children, but less than a year later he was expelled again and was back on the streets of Wilmington. He was 16.

With nothing to do one day, he took a bus ride to nearby New Castle Air Base, home to the Delaware Air National Guard. There, in a hangar, he got his first close-up look at an airplane. "It was a World War II P51 Mustang fighter," he wrote. "I was hypnotized!" After walking all the way around the plane, he climbed up on the wing and into the cockpit.

He was soon spotted by a guard, who yelled at him to get down. Frightened, he started to obey but was stopped, as a hand on his shoulder began gently pushing him back into the cockpit. Turning, he looked into the face of an Air Force captain wearing a flight suit. His name was James R. Shotwell, Jr. but, reported Dudley, "by the time I left the field that day he had become 'Jim.'"

During the months that followed, Shotwell spent many hours with the troubled teenager, introducing him to his Air Force comrades and encouraging him to turn his life around. But it didn't last long. His grandmother had had enough of his bad behavior, and he was sent to live with an aunt in Southern California. But Jim Shotwell wasn't about to give up and he wrote to Dudley often. "Those letters," he said, "brightened my days."

Then, on March 19, 1955, came the awful news that 33-year-old Shotwell had been killed when the engine of his plane quit and he crashed. He could have saved himself by ejecting, but was close to a populated area and refused to risk it. By the time he maneuvered to a safer place, it was too late to eject and he died on impact.

A Changed Life

Dudley, who'd been unwilling to change his ways, was devastated at the news. The only real friend he'd ever had, the only one who had treated him with so much kindness, was gone. But those seeds of kindness Jim Shotwell had planted in his mind began to take root. "I started to think of Jim," he wrote, "and the many things he had said to me. Instinctively, I was aware that something had changed. Now I knew where I was going in my life and what I would have to do to get there."

He spent the next four years in the Air Force and, after his discharge in 1959, went on to earn a pilot's license. Flying was now his life. He became a certified flight instructor and developed a talent in acrobatic flying. "By 1971," he wrote, "I had accumulated thousands of flying hours, flown more than a hundred air shows, and lectured all over the country to flight instructors learning the trade. During those years I flew just about everything, including some experimental and military aircraft."

Dudley Henrique retired from active flying in 1995, but his contributions to aviation have been by no means limited to his time in the air. He has written extensively on a wide range of aviation subjects, including flight simulation, air safety protocols, and the techniques of flying high performance aircraft. He has also donated countless hours to various organizations, including the Professional Race Pilots Association and the P51 Mustang Pilots Association, and he is a past president of the International Fighter Pilots Fellowship.

Jim Shotwell didn't live to see the results of his kindness but, in grasping the shoulder of young Dudley Henrique, he set in motion a series of events that would cause a troubled teenager's life to change and to bear fruit in ways he could never have anticipated.

From Slavery to Significance

Another boy whose life would be forever changed by an act of kindness was Frederick Bailey, born to a slave woman in 1818. He never knew his father and he was only seven when his mother left him with the owner of the plantation and his life of slavery began. He was beaten often and forced to go long hours with neither food nor sleep. Recalling those days, he would later write, "I was broken in body, soul and spirit."

Back then it was against the law to teach slaves to read and write, but the owner's wife, without her husband's knowledge, began teaching little Frederick anyway. It was a small and simple act of kindness, but it would change the boy's life, and the lives of countless others he would meet on his journey.

As a young man, he was determined to escape the life of a slave, and at age 20, he succeeded, moving to New York and then to New England. He married and began raising a family, but continued to pursue his education, something that would have been impossible without the kindness the plantation owner's wife had shown him.

To escape his past, and as part of his new life, he decided to change his last name to Douglass, and it was as Frederick Douglass that he would win renown nationally and internationally as a writer, publisher, and orator, and as a champion of the rights of slaves and of women. As an advisor to President Abraham Lincoln, he played a key role in the abolitionist movement. Later he would play a similar role in the women's suffrage movement.

During the Republican National Convention in 1888, as a measure of how far he'd come, he became the first African-American to be nominated as Vice President of the United States on the small Equal Rights Party ticket. While little more than a symbolic gesture, it demonstrated the power of a simple act of kindness. Frederick Douglass is remembered to this day as one of the most successful and prominent figures in U.S. and African-American history.

A Legacy of Kindness

Kindness, of course, isn't limited to the way that slave owner's wife or Jim Shotwell demonstrated it in reaching out to Frederick Douglass and Dudley Henrique. For example, consider the story of Agnes Bojaxhiu. Born in Macedonia in 1910, she had become a nun and was teaching at St. Mary's High School in Calcutta, India when she decided to pursue her dream. With permission from her superiors, she left the convent school to devote her life to working among the poorest of the poor in the Calcutta slums—beggars and children dying in the streets, dirty, unwanted, and ignored. So Agnes, who as a nun had become Mother Teresa, began a ministry she would continue and expand until her death in 1997.

She described her philosophy with these words: "Let no one ever come to you without leaving better and happier. Be the living expression of God's kindness: kindness in your face, kindness in your eyes, kindness in your smile." For nearly a half-century, she gave that unselfish, serving kindness to everyone in her path.

Mother Teresa never forsook her dream. Rather, she perpetuated it, starting homes for the poor, the dying, the leprosy laden, and the unfortunate throughout the entire world. A champion of the unwanted, the unborn, and the unloved—she traveled the world well into her eighties, with a challenge to the "haves for the have nots." The Missionaries of Charity, which she founded, now has more than one million workers, carrying on her labor of love in more than forty countries.

As an elderly woman, stooped with arthritis and barely 4'9" tall, Mother Teresa was asked how she felt being so bowed by her disease. Her response was classic: "It is not a problem, because I just get closer and closer to those I love."

She died with just five possessions: two robes, sandals, a bowl, and a Bible. But she died with a wealth of dreams realized and a Nobel Peace Prize, leaving a legacy of kindness beyond measure.

Lagniappe

Unless you've spent part of your life in the Deep South, you may not be acquainted with the word *lagniappe* (lan-yap). It describes a long-standing French-Creole tradition in southern Louisiana and parts of neighboring states. It's defined as a) a small gift given by a merchant to a customer with the customer's purchase; b) an extra or unexpected gift or benefit. It's often used to signify a small kindness or going the extra mile.

In his book *Life on the Mississippi*, published in 1883, Mark Twain wrote: "We picked up one excellent word — a word worth traveling to New Orleans to get; a nice limber, expressive, handy word — 'lagniappe.' We discovered it at the head of a column of odds and ends in the *Picayune*, the first day; heard twenty people use it the second; inquired what it meant the third; adopted it and got facility in swinging it the fourth. . . . It is something thrown in, gratis, for good measure."

I first heard about it from a mentor of mine, Naomi Rhode, one of America's finest public speakers and a past president of both the National Speakers Association and the Global Speakers Federation. In her book *My Father's Hand*, Naomi relates a story she often heard as a child from her father, a story I believe illustrates a unique way of showing kindness to others.

"My dad was a giant of a man," she writes. "His life philosophies, his character, his genuine zest for life, his charisma, his speaking excellence, his love for family, his wisdom, his storytelling ('to cement life's teachable moments,' he'd say), and his faith in God were the foundational elements of my childhood.

"Having lived through the 'Great Depression' in our country (about which he was always willing to share stories), he had a true appreciation of thrift. But far beyond thrift was a philosophy of giving. He'd often tell the story of the shopkeeper during the Great Depression:

> *"This shopkeeper was different than all the other shopkeepers in town. When you came into his shop to buy five pounds of coffee*

beans, he would take his marvelous scale and put a five-pound weight on one side and the empty container on the other. Then he would ceremoniously put the scoop into the bag of freshly roasted coffee beans, scooping and scooping until the once empty container was perfectly balanced with the five-pound weight.

The shopkeeper would then pause — and 'twinkle,' and dip the scoop into the bag of beans one more time. With a smile, he would empty that extra scoop of coffee beans on top of what he had so carefully measured, overflowing the container and tipping the scales in favor of you, the customer.

As he smiled and 'twinkled,' he would say 'Lagniappe,' which in French Creole means: 'every bit you paid for, and then just a little bit extra.' It was obviously that 'little bit extra' which had created, built and successfully retained the business other shops lost during that difficult time in our nation's history."

"In telling that story, my dad was extremely convincing! He assured me I would be happy, successful, and even significant in life's journey if I regularly gave 'every bit I was paid for, and then a little bit extra'—in my personal life, in my business life, with friends, and with family."

At the end of her dad's story, Naomi added these words: "What a wonderful model for all of us to follow in our lives: May each of us be a *Lagniappe* person, giving every bit we've been paid for, and just a little bit extra!"

The Ripple Effect

In New Orleans, among other places, the *lagniappe* tradition continues to flourish. For example, there are the Lagniappe Academies and Lagniappe Presbyterian Church. It's also the name of the magazine which has been published by the Junior League of New Orleans since 1930. In a recent issue of *Lagniappe*, editor Caitlin Brewster wrote about "following the theme of 'the ripple effect,' knowing that every little thing we 'Leaguers' do impacts someone or something else—no matter how big or how small."

She goes on to describe what happens when a pebble is tossed into a lake or other body of calm water: "Although the pebble is small, the effect is large. From that tiny *plop*, ripples begin to spread out in all directions. And it never ceases to amaze me just how far they can extend."

What a beautiful description of kindness. That's one of the great things about it—there's never a way to measure its effects. It can be something as simple as giving a dollar to that homeless man at the freeway exit, and perhaps go no further, or it can touch countless lives as it passes from one hand to the next. It also has a dual benefit, impacting both the one who bestows it and the one who receives it.

Avoiding the WIIFM Approach

If you set out to be a kinder person, which is a worthwhile goal for all of us, be sure it's for the right reasons. If you're just out to make yourself look good or if you expect to get something in return, that's selfishness rather than kindness. It's known as WIIFM, which stands for: "What's In It For Me?" While I admit in advance that the following is an extreme example, please don't follow the advice of Al Capone, the notorious Prohibition-era gangster: "You can get much further with a kind word and a gun than you can with a kind word alone."

No, no, Al! Pointing a weapon at someone while you hold out your hand for his wallet is definitely not kind, no matter how politely you make your request.

Speaking of pointing a gun, for more than a decade I've been a "SWAT Doc," initially with the Arizona Department of Public Service and, since 2003, with the Phoenix Police Department. The four physician members of the team go through SWAT Team training, physical fitness and handgun qualification. Although we're all armed, if we're the ones shooting, it will be a very bad day.

A few years back, I participated in the apprehension of a man with a solid—albeit illegal—business model. He'd rob other drug dealers at gunpoint (an Al Capone devotee) and steal their cash, weapons, and drugs. Not a bad business model. What are the victims going to do, call the police? His plan was ultimately discovered and he drew the ire of the police department. He was considered heavily armed, dangerous, and unpredictable.

Early one morning, eighteen of us loaded into three vans to storm the house of his girlfriend, where he was allegedly hiding out. As we approached the house, a neighbor heard him slapping his girlfriend around and called to report a domestic violence complaint. The sergeant in charge of the raid told the dispatcher not to send any help, as we were at that moment about ten seconds from "hitting his house." We pulled up, the vans emptied, doors and windows were breached and the bad guy was dragged out in tighty-whities without a fight.

I remember thinking about that neighbor who, out of concern and kindness, called the police for a domestic violence complaint and, seconds later, witnessed eighteen people, dressed in black Kevlar and carrying automatic weapons, storm the house, break in the windows, blow the doors off, and drag out the suspect. That neighbor must have been thinking, "Holy crap! They take domestic violence seriously here!"

Another American who became famous during the Great Depression was aviation pioneer Amelia Earhart, whose view of kindness was quite different than Capone's. "A single act of kindness throws out roots in all directions," she said, "and the roots spring up and make new trees. The greatest work that kindness does to others is that it makes them kind themselves."

———————— FOOD FOR THOUGHT ————————

- It's often the seemingly smallest acts that make the long lasting difference. Helping someone who's homeless, mentoring a younger person, donating your time and experience—these are simple things that mean a lot.

- It may not be altruistic to think like this, but I always get more benefit out of helping someone than he or she seems to; maybe it's because I typically get an extra dose of humility or perspective along the way.

IN OTHER WORDS

And now here is my secret, a very simple secret,
it is only with the heart that one can see rightly,
what is essential is invisible to the eye.
~ Antoine de Saint-Exupéry

Remember there's no such thing as a small act of kindness.
Every act creates a ripple with no logical end.
~ Scott Adams

I wonder why it is that we are not all kinder to each other than
we are. How much the world needs it! How easily it is done!
~ Henry Drummond

One of the most difficult things to give away is kindness –
it is usually returned.
~ Cort R. Flint

A kind heart is a fountain of gladness,
making everything in its vicinity freshen into smiles.
~ Washington Irving

The effects of kindness are not always seen immediately.
Sometimes it takes years until your kindness will pay off.
Sometimes you never see the fruits of your labors,
but they are there, deep inside the soul of the one you touched.
~ Dan Kelly

I expect to pass through life but once. If, therefore,
there be any kindness I can show, or any good thing I can do to
any fellow-being, let me do it now, and not defer or neglect it,
as I shall not pass this way again.
~ William Penn

Constant kindness can accomplish much.
As the sun makes ice melt, kindness causes misunderstanding,
mistrust, and hostility to evaporate.
~ Albert Schweitzer

Two important things are to have a genuine interest
in people and to be kind to them.
Kindness, I've discovered, is everything in life.
~ Isaac Bashevis Singer

Kindness is more than deeds. It is an attitude, an expression,
a look, a touch. It is anything that lifts another person.
~ C. Neil Strait

Kindness is a language which the deaf can hear
and the blind can read.
~ Mark Twain

So many paths that wind and wind;
When just the art of being kind
Is all this sad world needs.
~ Ella Wheeler Wilcox

You cannot do a kindness too soon,
because you never know how soon it will be too late.
~ Joan Winchell

CHAPTER

Learning: A Lifetime Pursuit

Being a learner is to recognize you don't know it all.
It also means you're open to change. It means to
actively continue searching for new ideas and thoughts
and to expand your own body of knowledge.
~ Sir Ken Robinson

I'm always amazed by the myriad of personalities encountered on any given day in the urgent care center or emergency department, at the office, or even when I'm simply out and about. Over the years, I've been fortunate to learn a few things from the thousands of patients I've treated and the remarkable individuals I've met along the way.

How is it that some people with serious acute or chronic diseases seem to accomplish so much, are very serene, and always upbeat? Why are some extremely accomplished individuals the most humble people you'll ever meet? How is it that some people never speak an ill word toward or about others?

I've often thought about the answers to these questions and others of the same genre. After more than 25 years in medicine and a half-century on this earth, I've come up with a few ideas.

So here's what I've learned:

Keep Learning

Socrates was quoted as saying, "A wise man knows he knows nothing." When you think about it, that's the best part of learning—the knowledge that there's still more to learn. How boring would life become if you knew everything you needed to know?

This list is far from exhaustive and, given some of my personal debacles of the past, I clearly have a long way to go during the homestretch.

Not long before his death at age 88, Michelangelo, the legendary sculptor and artist of Sistine Chapel fame, wrote two words on a sketch he had drawn: "Ancora imparo" — *I am still learning*. Imagine! This man, whose accomplishments few of us could even approach, remained eager to learn more, even in his old age. Keep in mind that when he died in 1564, reaching age 88 was *really* old!

I'm always inspired by stories of men and women who don't allow their advancing years to stop them from tackling something new. A well-known example would be a woman born in 1860 as Anna Mary Robertson who retired from her life of farming at age 76 and began a new career as an artist. Her married name was Anna Moses. From then until her death at 101 years old, she completed more than 1,600 —paintings and, as Grandma Moses, became one of our nation's most famous artists.

Like Grandma Moses, George Dawson was a centenarian who had decided late in life to learn something new. Born in 1898 as one of five children descended from slaves, his education ended at age eight when he began working on a farm. He held a variety of jobs until finally retiring at age 90. Six years later, he decided to do something he never had time for—he wanted to learn to read.

George learned well and, at age 98, he co-authored *Life Is So Good*, the story of his life. In June 2001, a month before his death, he wrote an article that appeared in *Guideposts* magazine. In it he wrote: "I'm still going to school, working on getting my GED, even though I'm 103. After all, now I know why I'm here. I'm here to learn. I'm here to help show folks it's never too late. . ."

There's the key to constant growth. Lifelong learning! It's what makes our journey through life richer and keeps us young. When your life becomes easy, complicate it. I love this comment by legendary automaker Henry Ford: "Anyone who stops learning is old, whether at 20 or 80. Anyone who keeps learning stays young. The greatest thing in life is to keep your mind young."

So, what's the first word that pops into your mind when you hear the word *learning*? Maybe it's *education, school, homework, graduation,* or that hard-earned *degree.* Does it bring back memories—unpleasant ones perhaps—of your days in the classroom? Or maybe you think fondly of those "School days, school days/ Dear old Golden Rule days."

That old song has been around for more than a century, but the part I remember is the line about being "taught to the tune of the hick'ry stick." In my case, the "hick'ry stick" was a ruler, applied rather frequently and painfully to the back of my head—by my kindergarten teacher!

That's right—in kindergarten! I remember as if it were yesterday: kneeling on hard linoleum in the corner of the cloak room, back straight, hands clasped together in front of me, eyes straight ahead, and then, WHACK, the sting of the ruler against the back of my head. I didn't appreciate it a bit at the time but, looking back, I'm sure Sister Marie Emelda, as arthritic as she was, meant well. Unfortunately, she had an unusually severe, Joseph Stalin-like way of demonstrating her compassion and charity toward all living things.

You may be wondering how having repetitive closed head injuries help? When things seem to be going not as planned, I can always say, "How bad can it be? At least a nun is not beating me senseless!"

Years later, I read Robert Fulghum's wonderful book, *All I Really Need to Know I Learned in Kindergarten*, and it dawned on me that corporal punishment, humiliation, and head injuries notwithstanding, I'd also learned some life lessons in kindergarten. In Fulghum's words: "Wisdom was not at the top of the graduate school mountain, but there in the sandpile at . . .school." They're lessons that have served me well, both personally and professionally.

"Clean up your own mess."

Nothing worthwhile is ever easy or without some messy situations. In business, making a mess of things occasionally is expected and probably necessary to move the business forward. There's one caveat, however. You need to stick around and clean up the mess. In other words, don't "pull a seagull"—swooping in, pooping all over everything, and flying away. Good leaders and good parents roll up their sleeves, as opposed to wringing their hands, and get dirty. Picking up the pieces helps you determine the root cause of the event, teaches you how to resolve it in case it ever happens again, and demonstrates to your team and your family that you lead from the front.

"Don't hit people."

Honestly, this is a tough one for me. Sometimes I think all that's needed is a good a** kicking to get an employee, or your child, back on the track. After all, look what it did for me during my prepubescent years. But Sister Marie Emelda aside, as much as you'd sometimes like to whap that person upside the head, there are better ways to address behavior which doesn't conform to your policies or culture. Identify the problem and make *it*, as opposed to the *person*, the issue for discussion.

At age three, my son Michael was a terrorist before it became somewhat commonplace. He was as stubborn as a mule, as strong as a little ox, and could scream like his arm was being cut off. One day when he was around four, I was so frustrated by him that, as he walked away from me during a discussion, I swatted him on his rear end, stopping him dead in his tracks.

Until that day, he'd never been spanked and this one "spank" caught him completely by surprise. He had a look on his face as if he'd just seen someone run over a squirrel in the road. Without missing a beat, he spun around and said, "Why is it okay for you to hit me, when you tell me not to hit others?" I have to admit that I was stopped dead in my tracks. I apologized, made no excuses, and never spanked him again.

"Say you're sorry."

As a business owner, a spouse, or a parent, apologies should come off your tongue easily, honestly, sincerely, and often. When your company doesn't live up to the expectations of your customers, apologize—even if their expectations are unrealistic. When you blame your son for leaving your car with an empty gas tank, and then discover your daughter was the last one to drive it, apologizing to him can set a good example.

By the way, I'm still waiting for Sister Marie Emelda to apologize. By my calculation, she's now 116 years old and is certainly too mean to die.

School Has Just Begun!

I'm sure Sister Marie Emelda and all the others who fell for that "Spare the rod and spoil the child" bit meant well, but it's no wonder that for most kids, the start of summer vacation was like getting paroled. We wouldn't even have to think about school for the next couple of months or so. I remember it well.

If you were like us, we dreamed of that day when we'd complete our formal education and could get on with living! It was time to take all that *learning* we'd accumulated and put it to work providing some return on those years we'd spent in classrooms.

But if you're wise, the learning process shouldn't stop the day you bid the campus farewell. That diploma or degree may testify that you've been educated, but education and wisdom aren't the same thing, nor are education and learning synonymous.

A Key Ingredient

Fair enough! But what's the secret, the primary ingredient, to being a lifelong learner? The answer, of course, is curiosity! The 18th century English author Samuel Johnson called curiosity "the thirst of the soul." Two centuries later American author William Arthur Ward described it as "the wick in the candle of learning." And the late, great Walt Disney claimed that it "keeps leading us down new paths."

If asked to nominate one person who, perhaps more than any other, might epitomize the word "curiosity," it would be hard to overlook the late Richard P. Feynman. He was a Nobel Prize-winning American physicist, scholar, and author, who served for many years as a professor at the prestigious California Institute of Technology, or, as it's popularly known, Caltech.

In many ways, Feynman belied the scholarly image of a professor and scientist and was better known in many circles as a prankster and practical joker. For example, while based at Los Alamos National Laboratory, where the atom bomb was being developed, he amused himself by picking the locks of cabinets containing top secret documents and leaving behind cryptic notes suggesting the presence of enemy agents.

At other times he taught himself how to juggle, play bongo drums, paint, and learn other skills with seemingly little if any connection to his scientific endeavors. Asked to explain what "made him tick," he told one interviewer: "I've been caught, so to speak—like someone who was given something wonderful when he was a child and he's always looking for it again. I'm always looking, like a child, for the wonders I know I'm going to find—maybe not every time, but every once in a while."

In two books he wrote, Feynman would go on to describe his never-ending search for such wonders. The first, *Surely You're Joking, Mr. Feynman,* was subtitled *Adventures of a Curious Character.* It was followed by, *What Do You Care What Other People Think?*, subtitled *Further Adventures of a Curious Character.*

It was his lifelong curiosity that enabled Feynman to reach the pinnacle of his profession and earn the respect of his peers.

The Questions You Ask

There are a couple of good ways to keep that wick of curiosity burning. One is by asking questions and another is by reading. Not long ago I heard a great story about a young boy named Martin Perl, who was born in New York City in 1927 to Jewish parents who had emigrated from Russia to the United States around the start of the twentieth century.

In his autobiography, Perl described the importance his parents placed on his education. "Going to school," he wrote, "and working for good marks, indeed working for very good marks, was a serious business. My parents regarded school teachers as higher beings, as did many immigrants. School principals were gods to be worshiped but never seen by children or parents. Parents never visited the school to talk about the curriculum or to meet with their child's teacher."

Yet it was his mother who instilled in him perhaps the most important lesson of all. "Every day when I came home from school," he explained, "she asked me, 'So, Marty, did you ask any good questions today?'" It was that habit of asking questions that helped Martin Perl become a distinguished physicist who, in 1995, was awarded the Nobel Prize in Physics for his discovery of the tau lepton—an elementary particle similar to the electron.

The Books You Read

Reading is another great way to continue the learning process. Back in Chapter 6, I introduced you to the late, great motivational speaker, Charlie "Tremendous" Jones. In addition to his speaking career, Jones was the CEO of Executive Books, a company he founded in Books were his passion and everywhere he went he'd proclaim: "You're the same today as you'll be five years from now except for two things, the people you meet and the books you read."

Over the years, his company, recently renamed Tremendous Life Books, has had cumulative sales well in excess of $100 million. He personally gave away countless thousands of books. "I hand them out instead of business cards," he said. "People may throw cards away, but they're unlikely to do the same with books."

In a long-ago letter to a young grandson, he offered this advice:

A proper diet is good for your body and the best books are good for your mind. Your life will be determined by the people you associate with and the books you read. Many people you'll come to love will be met in books. Read biographies, autobiographies, and history. Your books will provide all the friends, mentors, role models and heroes you'll ever need.

Biographies will help you see there is nothing that can happen to you that wasn't experienced by many who used their failures, disappointments, and tragedies as stepping-stones to a more tremendous life. Many of my best friends are people I've never met: Oswald Chambers, George Mueller, Charles Spurgeon, A.W. Tozer, Abraham Lincoln, Robert E. Lee, François Fenelon, Jean Guyon, and hundreds of others.

About reading, his message to just about everyone he met was the same: "Don't read to be big, read to be down to earth. Don't read to be smart, read to be wise. Don't read to memorize, read to realize. Don't read to just learn, read to sometimes unlearn. Don't read a lot, read just enough to keep yourself curious and hungry, to learn more, to keep getting younger as you grow older."

There you have them—the keys to becoming a lifelong learner: asking good questions and reading good books.

———— FOOD FOR THOUGHT ————

- Read, read, read. No matter the book, only good will come from it.

- Take classes—You need to get used to learning. Even if it's the most elementary or obtuse subject matter, you will get something out of it.

- Let your kids actively teach you. This gives them a situation within which to shine, let's you determine their progress, and allows you to be learner and a teacher.

———— IN OTHER WORDS ————

Ancora Imparo

~ Michelangelo

You can teach a student a lesson for a day;
but if you can teach him to learn by creating curiosity,
he will continue the learning process as long as he lives.

~ Clay P. Bedford

Learning should be a joy and full of excitement.
It is life's greatest adventure; it is an illustrated excursion
into the minds of the noble and the learned.

~ Taylor Caldwell

I began my education at a very early age –
in fact, right after I left college.

~ Winston Churchill

Get over the idea that only children should spend their time
in study. Be a student so long as you still have something to
learn, and this will mean all your life.

~ Henry Doherty

*Education would be much more effective if its purpose was
to ensure that by the time they leave school every boy and girl
should know how much they do not know, and be imbued
with a lifelong desire to know it.*

~ Sir William Haley

*The future belongs to the learners – not the knowers.
In times of massive change, it's the learner who will inherit
the earth, while the learned stay elegantly tied to
a world which no longer exists.*

~ Eric Hoffer

*Always walk through life as if you have
something new to learn and you will.*

~ Vernon Howard

*We never stop growing until we stop learning, and people who
are learning this simple truth will grow old but never get old.*

~ Charlie "Tremendous" Jones

I am learning all the time. The tombstone will be my diploma.

~ Eartha Kitt

*Never be too big to ask questions,
never know too much to learn something new.*

~ Og Mandino

*The best educated people are those who are always learning,
always absorbing knowledge from every possible source
and at every opportunity.*

~ Orison Swett Marden

*At the simplest level, only people who know they do not know
everything will be curious enough to find things out.*

~ Virginia Postrel

Never become so much of an expert that you stop gaining expertise. View life as a continuous learning experience.

~ Denis Waitley

*Life can be one dreary day after another
or a Baghdad of fascinating things to keep learning.
Get more out of every phase of your life –
stay incurably curious.*

~ L. Perry Wilbur

*Only the curious will learn and only the resolute
overcome the obstacles to learning. The quest quotient has
always excited me more than the intelligence quotient.*

~ Eugene S. Wilson

CHAPTER

Optimism/Enthusiasm:
Look on the Bright Side

Optimists are self-motivated by inspiring themselves to action. They believe in who they are and in what they are doing. They make mistakes and learn from them. They achieve success but don't take for granted that success will come again.

~ Ted W. Engstrom

I imagine that, at one time or another, you've read or heard various definitions comparing optimism and pessimism. Perhaps the oldest and most familiar one involves a glass of water (or other beverage), which the optimist describes as half-full, and the pessimist as half-empty.

Well, I recently heard of a young boy who turned that comparison upside down. After drinking half of his glass of milk, he set it down and announced: "I'm an optimist. My glass is half-empty." Told that his view was pessimistic, he replied: "Not if you don't like what's in it."

That's a pretty smart—and optimistic— kid, and I'm on his side. As I confessed in Chapter 7, I'm definitely an optimist, perhaps to a fault. Much of that is based on experience. I've found that, when something

---

seemingly doesn't go as planned, the outcome, more often than not, takes me down a previously undiscovered path. So at the end of the day, I've learned something, possibly gained a new perspective and usually have come out better. When it doesn't, I've discovered one more way not to do something and learned one more time that what doesn't kill you makes you stronger.

As I discussed earlier, I have failed—a lot. Looking back, out of each of those failures came some new learning, new growth, new perspective, more resilience, more education, more humility, and, most importantly, more funny stories. So, what's not to be optimistic about?

There is a downside to perpetual, blind optimism, though. It's when you fail to recognize a large impediment or barrier because you're so busy discounting its importance and looking only for the silver lining. However, don't swing so far that you fall victim to the Chicken Little (a/k/a Henny Penny) Syndrome, crying, "The sky is falling," whenever you encounter some minor mishap.

There's a world of difference between having an optimistic outlook and having a pessimistic one. Winston Churchill described that difference well: "The pessimist sees difficulty in every opportunity. The optimist sees the opportunity in every difficulty." He made his own attitude clear with these words: "For myself, I am an optimist — it does not seem to be of much use being anything else."

For Churchill, Britain's prime minister during its darkest days of World War II, it was that attitude, perhaps more than anything else, that served him and his people well. As the nightly Nazi bombings threatened his nation's very existence, it was Churchill's "Never give up" attitude that would help his countrymen not merely survive, but go on to defeat the enemy.

"What is our aim?" he asked. "I can answer with one word: Victory— victory at all costs, victory in spite of all terror, victory however long and hard the road may be; for without victory there is no survival." Under his inspiring leadership, victory was, indeed, finally attained.

The Choice Is Ours

What was it that made Churchill an optimist despite the terrible conditions he faced? He did the same thing every optimist does, and what you can do as well—he chose to be one! It's simply a matter of attitude and you control your attitude.

A great example is that of the late American journalist, author, and professor Norman Cousins. Among his many achievements was serving for 30 years as editor-in-chief of the well-respected *Saturday Review of Literature*. When he began that assignment in 1942, its circulation stood at a mere 20,000. Under his leadership, circulation grew to 650,000.

Cousins had been plagued with a variety of serious illnesses for much of his life, including heart disease and a rare form of arthritis. Yet, he maintained a positive attitude and outlook on life, once commenting: "Optimism doesn't wait on facts. It deals with prospects. Pessimism is a waste of time."

At one point, he became seriously ill and was hospitalized. When he asked about his chance of survival, the responses were grim, with one specialist telling him it was about one in 500, while another commented that he'd never seen a patient fully recover from that particular condition. Such a diagnosis might bring terror to the mind of even the most optimistic among us, but it had no such effect on Cousins.

Instead of resigning himself to that fate, he decided to take action. "Up until that time," he said, "I had been more or less disposed to let the doctors worry about my condition. But now, I felt a compulsion to get into the act. It seemed clear to me that if I was to be that one in 500, I had better be something more than a passive observer."

Cousins promptly checked himself out of the hospital and moved to a nearby hotel room, treating himself with large doses of Vitamin C and of laughter, the latter by watching as many old Marx Brothers films as he could find. "I made the joyous discovery that ten minutes of genuine belly laughter had an anesthetic effect and would give me at least two hours of pain-free sleep," he reported. "When the pain-killing effect of the laughter wore off, we would switch on the motion picture projector again and, not infrequently, it would lead to another pain-free interval."

Was this highly unorthodox form of treatment effective? Indeed it was! Cousins not only recovered fully, but he would live for many more years than his doctors had predicted.

Brother Act

It's one thing to use the power of optimism to dramatically improve one's health, as Norman Cousins did. It's quite another to use it as the foundation on which to build a $100 million company.

Meet Bert and John Jacobs, CEO and CCO, respectively, of New England-based *Life is good, Inc.* But don't let those initials fool you; they're not what you'd expect. Bert, the older by four years, is the company's Chief Executive Optimist and John is the Chief Creative Optimist.

The story begins in 1989 when the brothers, then in their 20s, decided to launch a T-shirt business, something they knew absolutely nothing about. Their "office," which did double duty as their "hotel room," was an old minivan with the back seats removed. Their meals consisted primarily of peanut butter and jelly sandwiches. Bert and John would hawk their wares on the streets of Boston and on college campuses in other East Coast locations. It was tiring door-to-door work, with little reward to show for it.

Driving back home from one typically unsuccessful road trip in 1994, they began lamenting the constantly negative reports that filled the airwaves and newspapers. They'd both graduated from college and began thinking it might be time to get "real jobs," as most of their classmates had done.

But they weren't quite ready to throw in the towel. "There has to be a way to send a more positive message to folks," they concluded. Back in their apartment, they gathered some friends to brainstorm ways to focus on the optimistic side of life.

Along Came Jake

One friend pointed to a drawing of a stick figure on their wall. It depicted the head of a beret-wearing, grinning stick figure John had drawn and had named Jake. "This guy's got it figured out," the friend said. That comment struck a chord, and the brothers quickly condensed it into three words: "Life is good."

The brothers took that sketch of Jake with the words "Life is good" below it, printed it on four dozen T-shirts, and headed to a street fair in Cambridge, Massachusetts. Forty-five minutes after setting up their display, every shirt had been sold. It was an eye-opening experience, in more ways than one.

In a profile of the company in the June 2012 issue of *SUCCESS* magazine, Bert described what happened. The first guy was a big strong Harley guy, all tattooed up and wearing a leather jacket. The second customer was a schoolteacher. She was prim and proper. The third person to buy a shirt was a punky kid with purple hair and a skateboard.

That experience sent a clear message to Bert and John that they'd hit on something that would appeal to a broad range of audiences. They quickly began introducing Jake to local retailers and that simple message of optimism spread far beyond what either brother could have ever imagined. Today, their company has grown to more than $100 million in annual sales and Jake's image appears on a variety of products for adults and children. The products are sold through some 5,000 retail outlets in the United States and in 30 other countries around the world. Says John: "We don't miss any demographics but we miss one psychographic—people who can't see the positive side of things."

Not content to simply build a large and profitable business, the Jacobs brothers have taken their message of optimism to another level. Bert explains: "'Life is good' has always been about spreading the power of optimism. One way we accomplish this is through our social mission, helping kids overcome life-threatening challenges."

Several years ago, the brothers launched the "Life is good" Kids Foundation, which supports extraordinary charities that create a lasting positive impact on children facing unfair challenges, including the trauma of violence, poverty, and loss. To date, it has raised millions of dollars to show those kids, in a tangible way, that indeed "life is good."

You may wonder how Bert and John managed to have such an optimistic view of life after five tough years of struggling, knocking on doors, sleeping in their van, and eating PB&J sandwiches, watching every penny. It would seem enough to discourage even the most cockeyed optimist.

Bert is quick to credit his mother for instilling a positive attitude in her children. "At dinner every night, my mother would start by saying, 'Tell me something good that happened today.' It was a great life lesson—and business lesson. By starting with what's good, whatever you focus on will grow."

The Electricity of Life

One characteristic that, in my experience, goes hand in hand with optimism is enthusiasm. That's certainly been the case with the optimists I've known and it's true in my life as well. In fact, "enthusiasm" is listed among the synonyms I found for "optimism."

One of my favorite definitions of enthusiasm came from a man named Gordon Parks. "Enthusiasm," he wrote, "is the electricity of life. How do you get it? You act enthusiastic until you make it a habit. Enthusiasm is natural; it is being alive, taking the initiative, seeing the importance of what you do, giving it dignity and making what you do important to yourself and to others."

What was it that made Gordon Parks an enthusiast? It certainly wasn't due to the conditions under which he was raised. Born in 1912, he was the youngest of fifteen children in a terribly poor black Kansas family. Conditions worsened when his mother died and, at age 15, he left home and dropped out of school. To support himself, he took on whatever job he could find. Thanks to a previously unrecognized musical talent, he taught himself how to play the piano and was hired to do so in a brothel. Later, he found work as, among other jobs, a busboy, waiter, semipro basketball player and big-band singer.

In his 20s, he happened to pick up a discarded magazine, and he was intrigued by the photographs he saw in it. Visiting a pawnshop, he spent $12.50 for a used camera. Thus began a successful career, which included 20 years as a photographer for *Life*, one of the nation's most popular magazines.

But Parks' accomplishments were by no means limited to photography. Turning again to his musical talents, he wrote the music for a ballet and composed a piano concerto. He wrote poems and a number of books, among them a novel titled *The Learning Tree*, based on his childhood memories. A movie based on the book was released in 1969 and was directed by him. It was the first time a Hollywood film was directed by an African-American.

His second film, *Shaft*, was released in 1971 and earned an Academy Award for one member of the cast. From then on, Parks would continue his activities in film, writing, and photography. In 1988, in recognition of his accomplishments, he was presented with the National Medal of Arts by President Ronald Reagan. Other honors continued to come his way, including more than 40 honorary degrees from colleges and universities in the United States and Great Britain. For a one-time high school dropout, Gordon Parks had indeed come a long way.

He'd been only 15 when his mother died, but he'd never forgotten the seed she'd planted that would grow and flourish, continuing to bear fruit right up until his death at age 93. "She would not allow me to complain," he once said, "about not accomplishing something because I was black. Her attitude was: 'If a white boy can do it, then you can do it, too—and do it better.'"

Raise Your Sights

Among the best-known proponents of enthusiasm and optimism in American history would almost certainly be Dr. Norman Vincent Peale. Dr. Peale, who died in 1993 at age 95, was a prominent New York minister and prolific author. His most popular book, *The Power of Positive Thinking*, was first published by Simon & Schuster in 1952, and over the years has sold some five million copies and has been translated into more than a dozen languages.

Two of his other popular books, also published by Simon & Schuster, were *The Tough-Minded Optimist* (1961) and *Enthusiasm Makes the Difference* (1967). In the opening chapter of the latter book, he writes, "Enthusiasm can truly make a difference—the difference in how your life will turn out. Consider, for example, the disparity between two current types. One group consists of the optimistic, the cheerful, the hopeful. Since they believe in something, they are the dynamic individuals who set events in motion, always working for the betterment of society, building new enterprises, restructuring old society and creating, hopefully, new worlds."

Summarizing, he called this group "energetic optimists," while describing pessimists as "purveyors of gloom."

For more than a half-century, Dr. Peale served as pastor of New York City's Marble Collegiate Church, which grew from 600 to more than 5,000 members under his leadership. In 1947, he and his wife Ruth helped launch what was then a four-page leaflet titled *Guideposts*. Today, it's among the largest magazines in the nation, with a monthly circulation of more than two million copies.

Norman Vincent Peale's legacy includes a word he introduced to our language and a challenge to all of us, perhaps most of all, to those who habitually drink from the half-empty glass. "I challenge you," he said, "to become a *possibilitarian*. No matter how dark things seem to be or actually are, raise your sights and see the possibilities—always see them, for they are always there."

Here's the take-home: there are people whose day-to-day existence is worse than the worst day of our lives. Yet they soldier on and make the best of their conditions, their illness, their trials, and their suffering. If they can do this, day in and day out—how can the rest of us not approach life with "can do" enthusiasm and unyielding optimism?

FOOD FOR THOUGHT

- If you're on the right side of the turf, how bad can it be?
- It's clear to me that, time and time again, optimism and enthusiasm have literally saved the day and sometimes the empire.
- Enthusiasm is infectious—spread it.

IN OTHER WORDS

One of the things I learned the hard way was that it doesn't pay to get discouraged. Keeping busy and making Optimism a way of life can restore faith in yourself.
~ Lucille Ball

Optimist: someone who isn't sure whether life is a tragedy or a comedy but is tickled silly just to be in the play.
~ Robert Brault

Flaming enthusiasm, backed up by horse sense and persistence, is the quality that most frequently makes for success.
~ Dale Carnegie

Few things in the world are more powerful than a positive push. A smile. A word of optimism and hope. And you can do it when things are tough.
~ Richard M. Devos

Enthusiasm is one of the most powerful engines of success.
When you do a thing, do it with all your might.
Put your whole soul into it.
Stamp it with your own personality.
Be active, be energetic, be enthusiastic and faithful, and you
will accomplish your objective.
Nothing great was ever achieved without enthusiasm.

~ Ralph Waldo Emerson

Don't ever become a pessimist ...
A pessimist is correct oftener than an optimist, but an optimist
has more fun—and neither can stop the march of events.

~ Robert A. Heinlein

Follow your enthusiasm. It's something I've always believed
in. Find those parts of your life you enjoy the most.
Do what you enjoy doing.

~ Jim Henson

Study the unusually successful people you know,
and you will find them imbued with enthusiasm for their
work which is contagious. Not only are they themselves excited
about what they are doing, but they also get you excited.

~ Paul W. Ivey

Optimism is the faith that leads to achievement.
Nothing can be done without hope and confidence.

~ Helen Keller

Catch on fire with enthusiasm
and people will come for miles to watch you burn.

~ John Wesley

Every memorable act in the history of the world
is a triumph of enthusiasm. Nothing great was ever achieved
without it because it gives any challenge or any occupation,
no matter how frightening or difficult, a new meaning.
Without enthusiasm you are doomed to a life of mediocrity
but with it you can accomplish miracles.
~ Og Mandino

Life's blows cannot break a person
whose spirit is warmed at the fire of enthusiasm.
~ Norman Vincent Peale

CHAPTER

Perspective: Changing It Changes Everything

Two men look out through the same bars;
One sees the mud, the other stars.
~ Frederick Langbridge

Life is simply about perspective. If ranked, this is the most important of all the lessons I've learned. Simply changing your perspective changes everything. For example, I recently had a patient who was in moderate respiratory distress from the pulmonary embolism we diagnosed in the emergency department. He was also dying of colon cancer. When I told him about this latest diagnosis, he said, "Whew, at least I'm still on the right side of the turf."

For most of us—me included—the thought of a pulmonary embolism would be horrifying. This man was afraid his colon cancer had metastasized to his lungs, so he was actually relieved when he heard the diagnosis.

Changing your perspective changes your attitude toward whatever life can throw at you. When all else fails to fix the problem, change your perspective.

Not Fun? Don't Do It.

In the grand scheme of things, we're only among the living for a short time. Why do things that don't bring you joy, or aren't fun? I'm continually amazed by people who hate their jobs, their lives, their significant others, their bodies, etc., but don't make any effort to change their circumstances. If they're unwilling to take the necessary steps, they should at least think about altering their perspectives, so that whatever's making them so miserable is seen with a fresh set of eyes.

From my perspective, I like to say I've never worked a day in my life. If you figure out a way to enjoy everything you do, then nothing feels like work. Winston Churchill said it this way: "Human beings are of two classes: those whose work is work and whose pleasure is pleasure, and those whose work and pleasure are one."

In the Control Room

Let's chat about a man who, over a 48-year career, experienced that happy combination of pleasure and work—for the most part anyway. His name was Charlie Jones (no relation to Charlie "Tremendous" Jones mentioned in chapters 6 and 9). As a well-known sportscaster, he spent nearly a half-century doing what he loved.

Born and raised in Fort Smith, Arkansas, Charlie began what would be an award-winning career in the broadcast booth, covering various sports for radio and TV stations in his hometown. In 1960, he joined the ABC network, broadcasting American Football League (AFL) games. In 1965, he moved to NBC, covering National Football League (NFL) games and numerous other sports until 1997.

Charlie's expertise was by no means limited to football. During his NBC career, he also broadcast the 1998, 1992, and 1996 Olympics; the 1986 FIFA World Cup (soccer); the 1991 Ryder Cup (golf); Major League baseball games; Wimbledon tennis matches, and other high-profile sports activities.

In introducing Charlie, I used the term "for the most part anyway" in describing his love for his work. One exception took place in 1996, when he first learned of his Olympic assignment. Instead of the high-profile events (swimming, track, etc.) he'd broadcast during the 1988 and 1992 Games (held in South Korea and Spain, respectively), his assignment in Atlanta was to cover the much less popular events of rowing, canoeing, and kayaking. Not only would they command smaller audiences, but they were to be staged at venues located miles away from the major events in Atlanta.

From Charlie's perspective, the assignment was a big disappointment. But he was a professional and wasn't going to allow his feelings to affect his work. Before the events got underway, he began interviewing the athletes who would be competing in them, asking them about how they might handle such conditions as rain, high winds, strong currents, and equipment malfunction. To his surprise, the answer to his questions, no matter which competitor he asked, was the same: "That's outside my boat." In other words, there was no point in worrying about things outside of their control.

Charlie took that lesson to heart, determined to put his feelings of disappointment aside and to give his very best to every event he broadcast. Later, he would rank his assignment at those Olympic Games among his all-time favorites.

But the lessons he'd learned from those athletes would have even greater impact in days to come. To capture those lessons, he teamed up with co-author Kim Doren to write a book, titled *That's Outside My Boat: Letting Go of What You Can't Control*. In their research they interviewed people from all walks of life about how they handle events outside of their control. The results, in the words of one reviewer, "reinforce the idea that focusing on what you can influence is what's inside your boat, allows you to relax, making for a less stressful, more positive, and ultimately more productive workplace and life."

Each of us has a control room in our minds. What takes place there is the same thing that changed Charlie Jones's attitude from disappointment to "by far the best Olympics of my life." In can be summed up in a single word—perspective!

The Almighty Customer

Ask anyone in business, from the proprietor of the corner convenience store to the CEO of a multi-national corporation, what the key to the success of that business is and the answer to your question is likely to be "customer satisfaction." Entrepreneurs and corporate executives brag about their customer service in such terms as "knock their socks off," "outrageous," "unexpected," "above and beyond," etc. The headline of a feature article in a recent issue of *SUCCESS* magazine (August 2012) proclaimed "The Customer Is King."

JetBlue Airways and other organizations publish a "Customer Bill of Rights" on their websites. From others, one often hears this well-worn statement: "The customer is always right." Marshall Field, the legendary retailing genius, understood the principle well. The story goes that he once overheard a clerk in his store arguing with a customer. "What are you doing?" he asked. "I'm settling a complaint," the clerk answered. "No, you're not," said Field. "Give the lady what she wants."

In retailing circles, there's an often-told tale of the consumer who brought a set of tires into a Nordstrom's store to return them and was given a refund, despite the fact that Nordstrom's doesn't carry tires. It may be mere legend, but it does burnish that organization's reputation for exceptional customer service.

But not everyone subscribes to "the customer is always right" theory. For example, the Padgett Thompson Division of the American Management Association rejects it completely. In a brochure promoting its "Knock-Your-Socks-Off" customer service workshop, the company says: "Forget it. Studies show that customers cause more than a third of the service and product problems they complain about."

The brochure goes on to say that top-notch service professionals don't "*pretend* the customer is right. They *make* the customer right."

A Different View

In the late 1960s, a couple of Texans, San Antonio attorney Herb Kelleher and a colleague named Rollin King, began to talk about launching a small airline that would operate only within Texas borders, serving the cities of Dallas, Houston and San Antonio. Various legal issues delayed their plan and it wasn't until 1971 that Southwest Airlines made its initial flight.

Kelleher had a different perspective on running a business than the typical entrepreneur has. While he recognized the importance of delivering quality service, the employee, not the customer, would be the top priority. Kelleher wisely recognized that well treated and well-satisfied employees would, in turn, treat their customers just as well.

Today the name Southwest has become synonymous with outstanding customer satisfaction, delivered by happy and often zany crew members who exemplify another of Kelleher's core beliefs: that the words "work" and "fun" are not contradictory but complementary.

Has the perspective Herb Kelleher brought to the airline industry been successful? While one business publication described his employees-first policy as apparent "business-school heresy," Kelleher says: "Your people come first, and if you treat them right, they'll treat the customers right, and the customers will come back, and that'll make the shareholders happy." Then he adds: "We have a People Dept. That's what it deals with, so don't call it Human Resources—that sounds like something from a Stalin five-year plan. You know, how much coal you can mine. We say everybody is a leader, no matter what your job is."

The results speak for themselves. As it nears its fortieth anniversary, it's America's largest domestic airline, with thirty-two hundred flights daily to more than seventy cities. What's perhaps the most impressive evidence of its success is that, in an industry known for its dramatic swings between profit and loss, Southwest has posted a net profit every single year!

The perspective that Herb Kelleher, who's now Southwest's Chairman Emeritus, brought to the company he co-founded continues to resonate throughout the organization—and beyond. In an article titled "The Best Advice I Ever Got" in its November 12, 2012 issue, *Fortune* magazine reported on a small survey it conducted, asking "21 luminaries from all walks—finance, law, tech, the military and beyond—for the one piece of wisdom that got them to where they are today."

Among these "luminaries" is Doug Parker, Chairman and CEO of US Airways. "In my case," he said, "it's not necessarily words of advice, but more advice I received through example. The example is Herb Kelleher, who I've gotten to know over the last 10 years.... . He is so good at listening and has really taught me how important it is to listen to your employees."

Lemons? Or Lemonade?

You've probably heard this century-old bit of wisdom about perspective: "If life hands you a lemon, make lemonade." Although it didn't originate with him, the late Dale Carnegie, well-known writer, lecturer and self-improvement guru, commented on it in his book *How to Stop Worrying and Start Living*. First published in 1946, the book is still in print today, with more than six million copies sold in dozens of languages.

"The fool," he wrote, "if he finds that life has handed him a lemon, he gives up and says: 'I'm beaten. It is fate. I haven't got a chance.' Then he proceeds to rail against the world and indulge in an orgy of self-pity. But when the wise man is handed a lemon, he says: 'What lesson can I learn from this misfortune? How can I improve my situation? How can I turn this lemon into lemonade?'" The answer, of course, is by a change of perspective.

In 2009, a 50th anniversary edition of another popular book about worry was released. Written by Dr. John Edmund Haggai, a contemporary Christian leader and author with over 60 years of service, the book is titled *How to Win Over Worry*. Like Carnegie's book, it has sold millions of copies in multiple languages.

In it, Haggai offers this insight, "The radar of worry sweeps far beyond the actual dangers and makes you believe that you're hemmed in on every side by problems you can't solve. Winning over worry begins with gaining proper perspective. . . . It all comes down to this: You choose to worry or you choose not to."

Worry—a futile and deadly exercise that throughout human history has claimed millions of lives. Yet despite hundreds of books warning of its dangers, it continues unabated. Google the word "worry" and you'll get about 499 million results.

With gazillions of words on the subject, Dr. Haggai summed it all up in just nine of them: "You choose to worry or you choose not to."

So what's it going to be for you—lemons, lemonade or, better yet, limoncello?

Fun in the Journey

Have you ever picked up a wedge of lemon and bitten into it to try and quench your thirst? If so, you know the "cure" is often worse than the disease. On the other hand, an ice-cold glass of lemonade on a hot summer afternoon is among life's pleasures.

The choice is yours; your journey through life can be fun. If it isn't, change the route, or change your perspective. I'm not sure I ever want to get to the destination. The struggle, the effort, the failures, the successes and the shared joy from the experience are what this is all about.

I don't think I've worked a day in my life. Don't get me wrong; there are days when I walk out of the Emergency Department after hours of treating the sick and the injured, or after having to fire a long-term physician. Those are times when I think they couldn't pay me enough to do these jobs. Thankfully, those days are few.

I've treated tens of thousands of patients. I've seen the look in the eyes of so many of them when they realize that everything they wanted to accomplish, everything they wanted to see, say, or do will be forever lost. The looks on their faces screams: "If only."

You should be enjoying the hell out of this life. If you aren't, change it. Don't wait until you're on your death bed saying "if only, if only." Don't waste a second.

FOOD FOR THOUGHT

- You alone have the power to change the course of your life. If you can't, and many believe they can't, at least change your perspective.

- Perspective changes as we age. What was once very important is now less important. Try to remember that when you need a perspective injection.

IN OTHER WORDS

What makes life easy or difficult or any other way we judge it for that matter is perspective. What matters most about your life and mine are not the objective facts or reality of it but rather the perspective from which we view it.
~ Roger Allen

*Focus on the journey, not the destination.
Joy is found not in finishing an activity but in doing it.*
~ Greg Anderson

Work is much more fun than fun.
~ Noel Coward

*There are things I can't force. I must adjust.
There are times when the greatest change needed
is a change of my viewpoint.*
~ Denis Diderot

I never did a day's work in my life. It was all fun.
(Thomas A. Edison
If you nurture your mind, body, and spirit,
your time will expand. You will gain a new perspective
that will allow you to accomplish much more.
~ Brian Koslow

If you can't be a highway, then just be a trail,
If you can't be the sun, be a star;
It isn't by the size that you win or you fail;
Be the best of whatever you are!
~ Douglas Malloch

Humor is perhaps a sense of intellectual perspective,
an awareness that some things are really important,
others not; and that the two kinds are
most oddly jumbled in everyday affairs.
~ Christopher Morley

What is funny about us is precisely that
we take ourselves too seriously.
~ Reinhold Niebuhr

Humor gives us balance and perspective;
it broadens our horizon and understanding; it makes us
come down from our high horse of arrogance and conceit.
~ Hyman Judah Schachtel

Perspective changes our attitude.
Changing our attitude breathes hope into us.
~ Bob Welch

CHAPTER

Indefatigable: Empty the Tank!

No one ever attains very eminent success by simply
doing what is required of him; it is the amount and excellence
of what is over and above the required that determines
the greatness of ultimate distinction.

~ Charles Francis Adams

What do I mean by "empty the tank?" Well, it's described in lots of ways: going the extra mile, and beyond; giving it all you've got; going for broke; and, to borrow a term from the popular poker game *Texas Hold 'Em*, going "all in," or betting your entire resources on winning. It's going above and beyond, to the absolute limits of your talents and strengths, over whatever barriers have kept you from becoming the best you can possibly be.

Most barriers are imaginary. Most people have greater capacity than they ever give themselves credit for. And most of us have never been truly tested. Some, sad to say, never get beyond simply doing what's required of them.

Think of people who run the Badwater Ultramarathon—135 miles in 120° heat— or Navy SEALs during Hell Week, or people who, against all odds, perform heroic feats to save others or themselves from catastrophe. If asked, probably very few of these outliers would ever admit to "knowing" they could have accomplished something that, up to that point, was unimaginable.

One such person is a woman named Pam Reed. To help overcome a 15-year-long battle with anorexia, this wife, mother, and entrepreneur decided to start running—and she hasn't stopped. She set her sights on entering, and completing, the Badwater event. It begins in mid-July in the Badwater Basin in California's Death Valley, 282 feet below sea level, and ends at the trailhead to Mount Whitney, 135 miles away and more than 8,000 feet above sea level.

In 2002 she not only entered and completed the event, she won it, finishing five hours ahead of her closest competitor. Then, to prove her victory was no fluke, she won it again the following year.

In her 2006 book, *The Extra Mile: One Woman's Personal Journey to Ultra-Running Greatness*, Reed described what it takes to empty the tank: "Runners are allowed up to 60 hours to complete the course. But if you want to finish among the leaders, you've got to cover the distance in *well* under a day and a half. That means no sleeping and minimal stopping. The winning time is usually in the range of 25 to 30 hours. In 2002, when I was the overall winner of the race, I set the current women's record of 27:56."

Out of Their Comfort Zone

In its January 2013 issue, *SUCCESS* magazine included an article titled "52+ Ways to Get Out of Your Comfort Zone," which included brief profiles of men and women who had learned how to overcome barriers in their lives and go on to empty the tank.

One item featured a woman named Cecilia Aragon who, as a child, was so afraid of heights that simply climbing a ladder caused her to break out in a sweat. Even the simple act of shaking hands with someone terrified her. To overcome her fears, she says: "I realized that if I was ever going to do anything, I had to expand my comfort zone pretty dramatically." Today, she's an award-winning computer scientist and university professor.

But there's a lot more to her story. As a graduate student, she swallowed her fear and accepted an invitation from a friend to take a flight in a small, four-seater airplane. During the flight, her friend challenged her to take the controls. It was a life-changing, empty-the-tank experience. As soon as the plane landed, she signed up for flying lessons. In 1991, within six years after her first solo flight, she was invited to join the United States Aerobatic Team. During her four years on that team, her skills as a daredevil pilot helped her amass dozens of trophies. Today she's among the world's leading aerobatic pilots, and I assume she's no longer afraid of climbing a ladder.

The *SUCCESS* magazine article also featured a 44-year-old Florida trial lawyer named Heath Eskalyo. As a child, he never was a swimmer because of his mother's nervousness about the water. Today, with the help of a coach, he's become an accomplished competitor in Ironman Triathlons. These events, which I think of as triathlons on steroids, require a 2.4-mile swim, followed immediately by a 112-mile bike ride, followed immediately by a 26.2-mile marathon. That's nearly twice the distance of an Olympic-class triathlon.

In the article, Eskalyo described what it's like to plunge into the ocean along with some 1,500 others: "It's a washing machine. You're going to be kicked, punched, elbowed." That's just the start of an event that will cover more than 138 miles—with no breaks. Those who finish, both male and female, earn the coveted title of "Ironman."

Up High at Show Low

Not long ago, I participated in my first triathlon in eighteen years, held in a town named for a card game. Show Low sits at 6,412 feet at the base of the White Mountains in northern Arizona. Remember the opening scene in the Academy Award-winning film *Chariots of Fire*, where a group of men are running barefoot, effortlessly, through the crashing waves on a beautiful beach, with the orchestra playing an inspiring melody in the background? (If you never saw the movie, or you've forgotten that scene, it's available on You Tube.) But in my case, it wasn't like that.

In complete contradistinction to *Chariots*, I staggered, blue and probably hypoxic, out of the water in the back of the pack. Once on the bike, I decided to pass everyone I could see ahead of me. I set my sights on a cyclist about 300 yards in front.

The words of the legendary multi-distance runner Steve "Pre" Prefontaine echoed in my mind: "A lot of people run a race to see who is fastest. I run to see who has the most guts, who can punish himself into an exhausting pace, and then at the end, punish himself even more."

I peddled faster. Hunched on the aero bars, I looked up and knew I could pass him. As I got closer, I realized something wasn't right. His bike looked different, he looked different, but I didn't care. I was gaining on him and that was all that mattered.

I zoomed past him feeling pretty damn good about myself. It was then I noticed: he had only one leg. Instantly, I knew who had more guts. That quickly brought me back to reality. With the rest of that long bike ride and the marathon immediately following it awaiting me, I had no reason to savor that one fleeting moment of triumph. However, I laughed at myself for the next 90 minutes that I was beaten in the water by a one-legged swimmer! How did he not swim in a circle?

But you don't have to be a stunt pilot or a superb (or mediocre) athlete to overcome whatever barriers may be keeping you from the potential within you. One of my favorite stories is about the 97-year-old marathoner. When asked how it was that he was still running at that age, he responded, "No one ever told me I shouldn't." If you admit to a barrier, it becomes one. Put more simply, you're not beaten until you quit.

Small Steps Become Giant Ones

This nation was founded by men and women for whom "emptying the tank" was a regular occurrence. The barriers they overcame to form the United States of America were astounding, costing many of them not only their fortunes, but their lives. That "Never give up and never give in" attitude is an integral part of our country's DNA, demonstrated again and again throughout American history.

For example, in a speech to a joint session of Congress on May 25, 1961, President John F. Kennedy announced a goal of putting an American on the moon and bringing him safely back to Earth before the end of that decade. It was a bold statement, as our nation had fallen well behind the Soviet Union in the so-called "space race."

The President ended his speech by describing the commitment that would be needed to reach the goal. He declared that it could not be accomplished, "unless every scientist, every engineer, every serviceman, every technician, contractor, and civil servant gives his personal pledge that this nation will move forward, with the full speed of freedom, in the exciting adventure of space." In others words, it would require that everyone involved would empty the tank in order to meet the goal.

Eight years later, in July 1969, Astronaut Neil Armstrong became the first human to set foot on the moon, uttering these never-to-be-forgotten words: "One small step for man, one giant leap for mankind." Shortly thereafter, Apollo 11 and its crew—Armstrong, Michael Collins, and Buzz Aldrin—returned safely to Earth. They, and countless others, had come together to make President Kennedy's challenging goal a reality.

The Reasons Why

For many, going the distance or emptying the tank is simply for personal reasons, to overcome internal barriers, and to challenge themselves, or to get out of their comfort zones and test the limits of their ability, strength, endurance and courage. They want to discover how far they can go.

Gordon Ritter, a venture capitalist and entrepreneur, is another of those profiled in the *SUCCESS* magazine article mentioned above. In college, he'd been a member of the rowing team and later took up mountain climbing. Included in his exploits was reaching the summit of Aconcaqua. At 22,837 feet, and part of the Andes mountain range in Argentina, it's the highest peak in South America.

A triathlete, he exercises vigorously and, according to the *SUCCESS* article, he "plans to tie a tractor tire to his waist and drag it around." By way of explanation, he says, "I continue to find ways to get out of my comfort zone. If you go too long without pushing boundaries, you do get stale."

Ralph Braun had a different reason for emptying the tank, and it began when he was merely six years old. Diagnosed with muscular dystrophy, his life expectancy didn't extend beyond his teen years. By age fourteen he was in a wheelchair. A year later, with his father's help, he built a motorized wagon to improve his mobility. By age 20, he'd built a motorized scooter from salvaged parts, which allowed him to get to and from his job at a nearby manufacturing plant.

Each time another obstacle was placed in his path, he responded. When the company where he worked moved farther away, he acquired a used Jeep which had been used to deliver mail and outfitted it with hand controls and a hydraulic tailgate lift. That allowed him to load and unload his scooter without help, and it eliminated any problems he might otherwise have had in getting to and from work.

Braun continued to invent ways to make travel easier for those with limited mobility. In 1970, he retrofitted a full-sized Dodge van with a motorized wheelchair lift, which he called the "Lift-A-Way." Word spread quickly and as orders began coming in, he quit his job and launched The Braun Corporation.

That was 40 years ago. In his 70s today, the man who wasn't expected to live past his teens oversees a company with more than 800 employees and is a world leader in the manufacture of wheelchair accessible vehicles and lifts. In 2012 President Barack Obama named him a "Champion of Change" for his contributions in bringing greater mobility to people all around the world.

Ralph Braun started it all as a way to help himself get around, but step-by-step and barrier-by-barrier, he kept emptying the tank and made the world a better place.

Let's Roll

There may have never been better examples of what it means to "empty the tank" than to consider the events of one of the most infamous days in American history—September 11, 2001. It's unlikely that anyone in this country who was perhaps aged six years or older on that day will ever forget it. The images of airliners deliberately flown into Manhattan skyscrapers and The Pentagon are permanently engraved in our minds, while the story of United Flight 93, which crashed into a Pennsylvania field that morning, brought new meaning to a simple two-word phrase, "Let's Roll."

Watching the twin towers of the World Trade Center burn and collapse, killing not only the occupants of those buildings but hundreds who had rushed to rescue them, was a terrifying sight. So many made the ultimate sacrifice that day, giving their all without a single thought of their own safety.

While we saw no images of the last minutes of United Flight 93, a brief recording of a passenger's cellphone call painted an equally heroic but tragic picture. With the crew of the plane already overpowered by terrorists, a few brave passengers led by Todd Beamer prepared to storm the cockpit and regain control of the plane. The final words captured by that cellphone call were his: "Are you guys ready? Okay, let's roll!" A few minutes later the plane crashed, killing all on board. As tragic as that was, the heroic "empty-the-tank" actions of those brave passengers foiled the plans of those terrorists to fly the plane into yet another crowded building.

Super Woman

On September 16, 2007, I had to do something I never, ever wanted to do, nor do I ever want do it again. It was a beautiful Sunday in Phoenix. I was sitting in my office with the door to the rooftop patio overlooking twin runways open to let in the warm breeze. I was taking a bit of a break and called Bill and Colleen, close family friends. Bill was a founding partner in a law firm where I am "Of Counsel."

By coincidence, he and I went to the same university. He graduated from law school the same year I started as an undergraduate, so we never actually knew each other while at Drake. As it turned out, I was hired as an expert witness on a case he was defending and we became fast friends. After I passed the bar exam, his firm hired me on a part-time basis to assist on medical malpractice defense cases. Over the intervening years, our family became even closer to Bill, his beautiful wife Colleen, and their four dynamic daughters.

On this particular Sunday, he told me his wife Colleen (an RN by training) was not feeling well. Her abdomen was bloated and her back hurt. She was 53. At this time, I had known Colleen for about seven years and had never, ever heard her complain—about anything. The fact that she didn't feel well, and told anyone, sounded ominous.

After some coaxing, I convinced them to meet me in the emergency department where, after a brief history and exam, I ordered a battery of blood work and imaging studies. Right after the CT scan of her abdomen and pelvis was completed, I ran up to the radiology suite to go over the study in person with the senior resident radiologist. I related the history and exam to her. She inquired why I was in casual clothes (shorts and a tee shirt) and why I was so interested. I hold her of our friendship and how I was concerned. She looked at me with large tears rolling down her cheek and said, "I'm so sorry, but I think your friend has metastatic ovarian cancer."

I know enough gynecology to know that particular diagnosis was a death sentence, and I was absolutely dreading having to share the news with Bill and Colleen. I went back downstairs, sat down, took Colleen's hand, and shared the news as gently as I could. She responded by thanking me, and apologized that I had to be the one to tell her. "I can only imagine how difficult this was for you," she said. In many ways, I'm glad I was the one who told her and, at the same time, that experience was the worst moment of my medical career.

Colleen died early in the morning on February 23, 2013. During the time from the diagnosis to her death, she absolutely emptied the tank—every day, every waking hour. She traveled the world and cared for her family and extended family—essentially everyone she has ever touched. She also started a foundation called Colleen's Dream (to support research for the early detection of ovarian cancer), and was a fantastic friend and role model to her four beautiful daughters—and everyone else.

Remarkably, as her body grew weaker, her determination and courage grew stronger. It wasn't necessarily her will to live; she knew she was dying and accepted it as well as anyone could who was given the diagnosis. It was her determination to set the bar high, to not for a moment indulge in self-pity, to encourage others, to exude grace, and to empty the tank.

She died with her four daughters sitting on her bed—at peace, with her face turned eastward. Early the next morning, before the world knew of her passing, her close friend awoke and immediately jotted down a poem which she sent Colleen's daughters in an email. It said, "Early this morning, I was awakened with a poem — I had no idea why, but it poured out already composed — and I feel certain Colleen was sending this to you.... I'm honored to be the messenger and please know I am holding you all in my heart."

Back to One

When my days of life have ended
And my time on earth is done
I'll lay my weary head down
And turn my face towards the sun.
I'll hold a thought of you, dear,
As my heartbeats slow to none.
I'll carry your love and laughter with me
On my journey back to One

~ Pam

Anyway

Emptying your tank, or going above and beyond, doesn't necessarily require such dramatic, daunting, or dangerous actions. There are probably few days that don't give us an opportunity to extend a kind word or a helping hand to someone else. Mother Teresa spent so much of her life doing exactly that, and she expressed her philosophy in these simple words:

- People are often unreasonable and self-centered. Forgive them anyway.

- If you are kind, people may accuse you of ulterior motives. Be kind anyway.

- If you are honest, people may cheat you. Be honest anyway.

- If you find happiness, people may be jealous. Be happy anyway.

- The good you do today may be forgotten tomorrow. Do good anyway.

- Give the world the best you have and it may never be enough. Give your best anyway.

- For you see, in the end, it is between you and God. It was never between you and them anyway.

---------- **FOOD FOR THOUGHT** ----------

- Most of us are fortunate never to have our capacity fully tested.

- I believe we always have much more capacity for love, tolerance, humor, kindness, strength, and endurance than we believe we do.

- When you think you're at the end, you're likely only about halfway.

---------- **IN OTHER WORDS** ----------

Refuse to throw in the towel. Go that extra mile that failures refuse to travel. It is far better to be exhausted from success than to be rested from failure.
~ Mary Kay Ash

Never forget that life can only be nobly inspired and rightly lived if you take it bravely and gallantly, as a splendid adventure in which you are setting out into an unknown country, to meet many a joy, to find many a comrade, to win and lose many a battle.
~ Annie Besant

When the morning's freshness has been replaced by the weariness of midday, when the leg muscles give under the strain, the climb seems endless, and suddenly nothing will go quite as you wish – it is then that you must not hesitate.
~ Dag Hammarskjöld

Most of our obstacles would melt away if, instead of cowering before them, we should make up our minds to walk boldly through them.
~ Orison Swett Marden

*If you want to take your mission in life to the next level,
if you're stuck and you don't know how to rise,
don't look outside yourself. Look inside.
Don't let your fears keep you mired in the crowd. Abolish
your fears and raise your commitment level to the point of no
return, and I guarantee you that the champion within will
burst forth to propel you toward victory.*

~ Bruce Jenner

*I want to dare you to start a crusade in your life –
dare you to be your best. The only reason you are not the person
you should be is you don't dare to be. Once you dare, once you
stop shifting with the crowd and face life courageously, life
takes on a new significance. New force takes shape within you.*

~ Charlie "Tremendous" Jones

*It's only when we truly know and understand that we have a
limited time on earth—and that we have no way of knowing
when our time is up—that we begin to live each day to the
fullest, as if it was the only one we had.*

~ Elizabeth Kubler-Ross

*I am here for a purpose and that purpose is to grow into a
mountain, not to shrink to a grain of sand. Henceforth will
I apply ALL my efforts to become the highest mountain of all
and I will strain my potential until it cries for mercy.*

~ Og Mandino

*Dare to be what you ought to be; dare to be what you dream to
be; dare to be the finest you can be. The more you dare, the surer
you will be of gaining just what you dare!*

~ Norman Vincent Peale

Life is not a journey to the grave with the intention of arriving safely in a pretty and well-preserved body, but rather to skid in sideways, thoroughly used up, totally worn out, and loudly proclaiming 'Wow! What a ride!'

~ Peter Sage

There are no traffic jams along the extra mile.

~ Roger Staubach

CHAPTER

Efficiency: Doing Better What's Being Done

*By concentrating our efforts upon a few major goals,
our efficiency soars, our projects are completed,
we are going somewhere.*

~ Michael Korda

Have you ever met people who just seem to get more done in the day than everyone else? They never seem harried or stressed, or even busy. Yet their output is over the top. They must know something the rest of the world doesn't about efficiency—how to be as productive as possible, given the time and resources available.

For example, how is it that Theodore Roosevelt accomplished so much during his relatively brief lifetime? He died in 1919 at age 59—long before the Age of Technology—but his record clearly reveals a man who was ahead of his time and always on the go. In a 2006 profile of him in *TIME* magazine, he was called "The 20th Century Express," and a brief look at just some of his achievements confirms the accuracy of that description.

Among his accomplishments:

- The first President to fly in an airplane, to dive in a submarine, to own an automobile, and to have a telephone in his home.

- The first President to travel outside the borders of the U.S. while in office. He took the battleship USS Louisiana to Panama in 1906.

- The first President to entertain an African-American (Booker T. Washington) in the White House.

- The first American to win a Nobel Prize in any category, receiving the Nobel Peace Prize in 1906.

- The president who signed into law the first 51federal bird sanctuaries and the first 18 national monuments.

- He was a state legislator, police commissioner, and governor in New York.

- Owned and worked a ranch in the Dakotas.

- Served as Assistant Secretary of the Navy.

- Fought as leader of the Rough Riders in the Spanish-American War and was posthumously awarded the Medal of Honor.

- Served as President for two terms, then later ran for an unprecedented third term.

- Wrote more than 35 books, the first while he was only 24.

- Read tens of thousands of books, including several a day in multiple languages.

- Explored the Amazonian rainforests.

- Discovered and navigated the completely uncharted Amazonian River of Doubt, over 625 miles long; its name was later changed to Rio Roosevelt.

- Volunteered to lead a voluntary infantry unit into WWI at age 53.

- Maintained a strenuous lifestyle, and actively participated in boxing, tennis, hiking, rowing, polo and horseback riding (among other things).

• Remains the youngest man ever inaugurated as President.

Just reading that list can make me tired. Measuring your output by Roosevelt's standards makes all of us appear inefficient and underperforming.

A Better Way

Let's take a closer look at exactly what we mean by "efficiency," which is sometimes confused with the word "effectiveness." Both words are used frequently in the management literature, and some dictionaries even show each as a synonym of the other. In fact, they have separate meanings.

Probably the most succinct statement about their difference came from the late Peter Drucker, the best known and most respected management consultant, educator and author of the twentieth century. Here's what he said: "Efficiency is doing things right; effectiveness is doing the right things." Both are important management tools and they're not contradictory but complementary. While Drucker ranked the second as somewhat more important, he also said: "Efficiency is doing better what is already being done."

Among the best examples I know of someone "doing better what is already being done" is a man named Frederick W. Smith. Born in Mississippi in 1944, he developed an early love for flying and by the time he was a teenager he had earned his license as an amateur pilot. During his four years at Yale University in Connecticut he continued his interest in flying, serving as a charter pilot at the Tweed-New Haven airport.

It was during that time that an idea began to take shape in young Fred Smith's mind. Other pilots he met kept talking about the inefficiencies they experienced in delivering parts and equipment. In a 2004 interview with *Business Week* magazine, he made what he called "a very simple observation. As society automated, as people began to put computers in banks to cancel checks—rather than clerks—or people began to put sophisticated electronics in airplanes—society and the manufacturers of that automated society were going to need a completely different logistics system."

It was that observation which led him to write an economics class paper outlining what he saw as a need for developing an overnight delivery service in the rapidly growing computer age and his plan for meeting that need. In other words, he envisioned what Peter Drucker had defined as a way of doing better what was already being done.

It was that class paper which has become the stuff of legend. Supposedly, Smith's professor had given the paper a "C" and commented that such a plan wasn't feasible. Smith himself doesn't remember either the grade he received or any comments about it by his professor.

After graduation in 1966 from Yale, where he'd been in the U.S. Marine Corps training program, he joined the Marines, and during the course of the next four years, he served two tours of duty in Vietnam. He was not a Marine pilot, but flew with pilots as a forward air controller on more than 200 combat missions. During his four-year career, he paid close attention to procurement and delivery procedures, as his dream continued to grow.

In 1970, after completing his military service, Smith acquired an interest in an aircraft maintenance company and a year later, confident he could do more efficiently something that was already being done, he launched Federal Express Corporation. In that same *Business Week* interview he noted that the situation had gotten worse, as others "were trying to use an infrastructure built around mostly passenger air transportation—the airlines—which wasn't designed to handle it at all."

Today Smith serves as chairman, president, and CEO of what became simply FedEx, a company with more than 300,000 team members operating in more than 220 countries. Its fleet of some 700 planes and 80,000 land vehicles handle nine million shipments—every day! With annual revenues in excess of $42 billion, FedEx is among the one hundred largest companies in the United States and is consistently ranked as one of the world's most admired companies. And it all began when a young man took note of an inefficient system, knowing there had to be a better way.

Put It in Writing

One of the best ways to become more efficient in every area of your life is to set goals for yourself. I'm not talking about pipe dreams or bucket lists or wish lists. I'm talking about what are known as **S.M.A.R.T.** goals, goals which are Specific, Measurable, Achievable, Realistic, and Time-bound. And they must be written goals. As well-known speaker, consultant, and author Tom Hopkins advises: "An unwritten want is a wish, a dream, a never-happen. The day you put your goal in writing is the day it becomes a commitment that will change your life. Are you ready?"

Of course, having those goals won't do us much good unless we take the next step and act on them. In his award-winning book, *Moving from Activity to Achievement*, author/speaker Les Taylor writes: "Actions are those specific tasks we must accomplish in order to achieve our goals. Actions, like goals, must be measurable but, unlike goals, are proximate, short-term and quickly accomplished."

Putting those tasks in writing, such as making "to-do lists," is an especially good way to become more productive and efficient. That principle is perhaps best illustrated

by a century-old story that has become famous in business circles. It involved high-rolling and flamboyant Charles M. Schwab, CEO of Bethlehem Steel Corporation and a man named Ivy Ledbetter Lee, considered by many a founder of modern public relations. He was also what was then popularly known as an "efficiency expert."

It was in that capacity that Lee, aware of Schwab's interest in improving his own efficiency and that of his management team, approached him.

He told Schwab he could accomplish that goal simply by spending a few minutes with each manager. When asked what his fee would be, Lee replied that it would cost Schwab nothing, he was simply asking that the system he would suggest be tried for three months. At that point, Schwab would pay him whatever he felt it was worth.

Lee's advice was simple. Each person was to write a list of his most important tasks and number them in order of importance. Each task was to be tackled in that order—and completed—before moving to the next one. Unfinished tasks at day's end would be moved to the following day's list. All the participants agreed to follow Lee's plan for three months. At the end of that period, Schwab was so impressed by the results that he reportedly sent Lee a check for $25,000, equal to many times that amount today.

The Age of Technology

We don't have to look very far these days to recognize the enormous impact technology has had on virtually every facet of our lives. Many of the changes we've seen have helped us run our lives and our organizations more efficiently than ever before. Many of today's giant companies—Apple, Microsoft, Amazon, Dell, Facebook , and so many others—didn't even exist a generation or so ago. Today we can do our banking, pay our bills, buy our groceries (and just about everything else we need), conduct our meetings, see a doctor, and visit with family and friends—all without having to leave our homes or our offices. Technology may or may not have made our lives easier, but has certainly provided the tools to make us more efficient.

One of the most amazing stories began on January 12, 1964, when Jeffrey Preston Jorgensen was born in Albuquerque, New Mexico. As a young teenager, his dream was to become an astronaut, and he finished high school as class valedictorian. His next stop was Princeton University, where he planned to major in physics, but then switched to computer science. In 1986, he graduated *summa cum laude* with a Bachelor of Science degree in electronic engineering and computer science.

With degree in hand, he headed to New York, beginning a brief but very successful career in banking. Computer science remained his first love, however, and at age 30 he launched his own company, named Cadabra. Within just a few years that young man and his company would achieve worldwide success and fame.

At this point, you may be asking yourself: "Why haven't I ever heard of either Jeffrey Jorgensen or a company named Cadabra?" Well, it's confession time, so let me clear things up for you. Not long after Jeffrey was born, his parents divorced, and five years later his mother married a man named Miguel Bezos, who legally adopted her young son. As for the name Cadabra, Jeff Bezos changed it in 1995—to Amazon. In true entrepreneurial fashion, Bezos started his company in his garage in Seattle. Today, as Chairman and CEO, he oversees a company with 56,000 employees, serving more than 160 million customers around the world. What began as a small online bookseller now has more than twenty million products in stock, ready to be shipped as soon as the orders come in. Amazon, started less than 20 years earlier, has become the Internet's largest retailer.

What's behind such incredible growth? The answer, of course, lies primarily with its founder, whose passions are serving customers and continually improving efficiency. In 1999 when his company was just five years old, *TIME* magazine chose Jeff Bezos as its "Person of the Year." In an article in that issue, Microsoft's Bill Gates had this to say about him: "He understood from the beginning that he wasn't just inventing a new and more efficient way for people to find the books they wanted to buy, but that he was also helping to define a fundamentally new way to conduct a consumer retail business."

For Bezos, customer service and efficiency go hand in hand. In a recent article in *SUCCESS* magazine (August 2011), two quotes make that clear. "Our vision," he said, "is to be earth's most customer-centric company, to build a place where people can come to find and discover anything they might want to buy online." The book business remains a key part of Amazon's business and Bezos' goal is to "sell every book ever printed, in any language, in and out of print, in less than 60 seconds."

Let's see—products: every book ever printed; target market: everywhere on earth; delivery time: less than 60 seconds. Any questions?

How Sweet it Is

The concept of "efficiency" certainly isn't new. There's another giant company where efficiency is a primary goal, a company that's been around quite a bit longer than Amazon. In fact, the seeds that grew to become Mars, Incorporated were planted in the late nineteenth century in the kitchen of a home in Hancock, Minnesota. It was there that Alva Mars began teaching her young son, Franklin, how to hand-dip candy.

Franklin, who became better known as Frank, proved to be a good student and, in 1902, when he was 19-years-old, he began selling molasses chips. In 1910, he founded the Mars Candy Company in Tacoma, Washington. It enjoyed early success but went out of business a few years later. Undeterred, Frank Mars moved his young family to Minneapolis and, in 1920, he founded the Mar-O-Bar Company, which was incorporated three years later as Mars, Incorporated.

By then, Frank's son Forrest had become active in the business and it was at his suggestion that the company introduced what became the famous *Milky Way* candy bar. Other products followed, including *Snickers* and *M&Ms*, as the company continued to grow and prosper.

Today, Mars is a worldwide company, which is still 100 percent owned by the Mars family and ranked by *FORBES* as the third largest privately owned company in the United States. Based now in McLean, Virginia, it has 72,000 employees and completes an estimated 200 million consumer transactions—every day! Its global revenues exceed $30 billion dollars a year.

What accounts for such outstanding success, sustained for the better part of a century? The answer to that question can be found on the company's website: "Our strength lies in our efficiency, the ability to organize all our assets—physical, financial and human—for maximum productivity. In this way, our products and services are made and delivered with the highest quality, at the least possible cost, with the lowest consumption of resources; similarly, we seek to manage all our business operations with the most efficient processes for decision making."

Efficiency is one of "The Five Principles of Mars," the others being Quality, Responsibility, Mutuality, and Freedom. These principles, company officials report, "are the foundation of our culture and our approach to business. They unite us across geographies, languages, cultures and generations. Our Five Principles are synonymous with Mars and have been guiding Mars Associates throughout most of our company's history." Visit any of Mars' 400 manufacturing facilities and offices, located in 73 countries, and you'll find "The Five Principles of Mars" prominently displayed.

On a Personal Note

Having looked at these giant companies and the role efficiency has played in their growth and success, I don't want to minimize its importance in much smaller settings as well. Based on my own experience in the field of emergency and urgent care medicine, and as a pilot, I can testify to its importance. When you observe a pilot or a surgeon in action, you'll see that the ones who are the most adroit make the least number of moves, corrections, and control inputs. Their hands glide effortlessly over the controls or instruments. They have economy of movement, thus conserving energy and enhancing their efficiency.

While efficiency can have life or death consequences in either field, many of the lessons I've learned can be applied in a wide range of situations, large or small. Here are just a few suggestions you may find helpful in becoming more efficient—whatever the task:

- **Preparation:** Do your homework
- **Anticipation:** Murphy may be right around the corner
- **Focus:** It's easy to get distracted, especially in routine matters
- **Flexibility:** The best laid plans…
- **Limitations:** None of us is as smart as all of us
- **Communication:** Everyone on the same page
- **Delegation:** Be ready to pass the baton

FOOD FOR THOUGHT

- I'm sure you've noticed some recurring themes: Put it in writing, use a checklist, press on when you feel like quitting, and stay positive—it *will* work, you *will* learn, and you *will* have fun!

- It's much easier to be efficient when you're having fun. When you're not having fun, change your course or change your perspective.

IN OTHER WORDS

*The most efficient way to live reasonably is
every morning to make a plan of one's day
and every night to examine the results obtained.*

~ Alexis Carrel

*There is never an open road, except the road that leads to
failure. Every great success has always been achieved by fight.
Every winner has scars…. The men who succeed are the
efficient few. They are the few who have the ambition and
willpower to develop themselves.*

~ Herbert N. Casson

Efficiency is doing things – not wishing you could do them,
dreaming about them, or wondering if you could do them.
~ Frank Crane

There can be no economy where there is no efficiency.
~ Benjamin Disraeli

Loyal and efficient work in a great cause, even though it may
not be immediately recognized, ultimately bears fruit.
~ Jawaharlal Nehru

Do not be awestruck by other people and try to copy them.
Nobody can be you as efficiently as you can.
~ Norman Vincent Peale

A particular shot or way of moving the ball can be
a player's personal signature, but efficiency of performance
is what wins the game for the team.
~ Pat Riley

The higher your energy level, the more efficient your body.
The more efficient your body, the better you feel and the more
you will use your talent to produce outstanding results.
~ Anthony Robbins

It is more than probable that the average man could, with no
injury to his health, increase his efficiency fifty percent.
~ Walter D. Scott

Make yourself an efficient spark plug,
igniting the latent energy of those about you.
~ David Seabury

CHAPTER

Integrity: A Priceless Commodity

A reputation for integrity is your most valuable commodity.
If you try to put something over on someone,
it will come back to haunt you.
~ Victor Kiam

Simply put, integrity is doing what you say and saying what you'll do. The term is derived from the Latin word *integer*, which means "whole or complete." When a person has integrity, he or she is believed to have an inner sense of "wholeness," derived from consistency of action and character. The characteristics or qualities that comprise integrity are often defined as truthfulness, honesty, consistency, morality, accountability, responsibility, and loyalty.

Today's media is filled with stories that lead to the almost inevitable conclusion that integrity is sorely lacking in our nation and around the world. From swindlers to pedophiles, identity thieves to drug-using athletes, from prevaricating politicians to philandering spouses, virtually every facet of society has been infected by predators preying on innocent victims.

While integrity today seems to be lacking to a greater degree than ever before, we should keep in mind that it's been going on throughout recorded history. Before we throw in the towel, however, let's look at some examples which indicate that integrity is still alive and well in many circles.

On second thought, when we consider how much attention is paid when someone demonstrates integrity, "alive and well" may be an over-statement. Were that really the case, the two stories I'm about to tell likely wouldn't have attracted much attention.

A Tennis Match

Unless you're an avid tennis fan and have been for a long time, the name Eliot Teltscher may not be familiar to you. The son of immigrants from Israel, he was born in Southern California in 1959. Encouraged by his parents, he began playing tennis at age nine.

It proved to be a good choice. By the time Eliot was 17, he was among the top ten junior players in the nation. That performance earned him a tennis scholarship at the University of California at Los Angeles (UCLA). In his only year at UCLA (1978), he was named an All-American.

Teltscher left UCLA to become a professional tennis player and, within a year, he was ranked among the top ten players in the world. Known as a fiery competitor, he retired as a player in 1988 to become a tennis coach.

When asked which of his many accomplishments he's most proud of as a tennis player, it's not his many victories or awards he first mentions. In fact, it was in a moment of defeat that his competitive nature was overruled by his integrity. In 1982, playing another top-ten ranked player, Vitas Gerulaitis, in the final round of a major tournament, the latter was at match point. Gerulaitis then hit a shot that barely cleared the net, seemingly out of Teltscher's reach, but at the last second he was able to reach the ball and lob it over his opponent's head, staving off defeat, at least momentarily.

However, Teltscher knew something that neither his opponent nor the umpire realized. In his lunge to retrieve the ball, his racket had barely scraped the net, in violation of the rules. It had no effect on his shot, nor would anyone have been the wiser. But Eliot Teltscher was and he immediately reported the infraction, costing him not just that point but the match as well.

Some 2,500 years ago, the Greek philosopher Heraclitus wrote: "Good character is not formed in a week or a month. It is created little by little, day by day." Teltscher's immediate reaction and response wasn't something he had to think about. It was his integrity that shaped his life and revealed itself in an instant.

"Because that's what we do."

Over the years, the one sport that has seemed to avoid most of the scandals, which have plagued other sports, is golf. Now, I'm not talking about the personal lives of prominent golfers, but about how the sport itself is played. For example, golf is the only popular sport in which there are no referees overseeing the action on the course; the players themselves are responsible for playing by the rules and for penalizing themselves for any sort of violations of those rules, whether those violations are seen by others or not.

Imagine a baseball game without umpires, where each pitch would almost certainly trigger a heated debate between pitcher and batter. The games would go on endlessly. The golfer, by contrast, is his own official, responsible for following the rules—no mean feat by the way, judging by the size and complexity of golf's official rule book.

Over the years, there have been widespread reports of golfers calling penalties on themselves, often for infractions of which no one else is aware. In addition to perhaps a one-stroke or two-stroke penalty, the financial consequences can be enormous. That golfers will do it regularly is a testimony to the standards of integrity present on the golf course.

One of the most vivid recent infractions involved a British golfer named Brian Davis, who called a penalty on himself for an infraction he wasn't even certain he had committed. Nevertheless, he not only called attention to it, but insisted that TV replays be reviewed to decide the matter.

Davis, who was born in London in 1974, became a professional golfer in 1994. He played primarily on the European tour until 2006, when he decided to join the PGA tour here in the U.S. While he had won a couple of tournaments in Europe, he had yet to win a PGA event.

He came close to his first victory on American soil in 2010, when he sank a long putt on the 72nd hole of the Verizon Heritage Classic in Las Vegas to tie Jim Furyk for the lead, forcing a "sudden death" playoff. On the first playoff hole, Furyk was on the green with his second shot, while Davis's shot was in a hazard. After reaching the green on his next shot, Davis felt he might have inadvertently brushed a loose reed on his back swing, a two-stroke penalty.

No one, including Davis, saw it happen, but he called over an official and asked to have the shot replayed on a nearby TV camera. The real time review showed nothing and Davis would have been well within his rights to continue play, but he insisted the shot be shown again in slow motion. Almost imperceptibly, it showed that his clubhead had barely brushed a reed and hadn't impacted his swing in any way. However, that reed—or "a loose impediment" in golf terminology— had indeed moved, incurring a two-stroke penalty.

Davis immediately called that penalty on himself, ending the playoff, and resulting in a victory for Furyk. The difference in prize money between first and second place was $400,000! But Davis was quick to point out that a great deal more was at stake than the prize money. "No," he said. "It probably cost me more like $2 million. A win would've gotten me into the Masters. My endorsement bonuses would have kicked in. A win opens so many doors…. There's no price you could put on it. It cost me $400,000 on that Sunday. But how much did it really cost me? Who knows? Winning at the Verizon Heritage would've been awesome. Probably the hardest thing is knowing how much a win can possibly change your career."

Asked if he thought about all that before insisting on the review, he said, "No. I thought I saw something move and I wanted to check. Because that's what we do. That's what golfers do."

The late Grantland Rice was perhaps the most famous and well respected sportswriter of the first half of the twentieth century. Golf was among his favorite sports and he once said: "Eighteen holes of match play will teach you more about your foe than eighteen years of dealing with him across a desk." That's a test of integrity Brian Davis would have easily passed.

A Look in the Mirror

If you're a football fan, you may recognize the name John McKay. McKay was a prominent football coach who, after a successful college coaching career at the University of Southern California, was recruited to become the first head coach of the Tampa Bay Buccaneers in 1976, when that team began play in the National Football League (NFL).

McKay was very popular with the media because he could nearly always be counted on for a quotable comment or two during his post-game interviews. Many of his comments were humorous or sarcastic, but one of my favorites is about integrity. Here's what he said: "I am a big believer in the 'mirror test.' All that matters is if you can look in the mirror and honestly tell the person you see there that you've done your best."

In mentioning the "mirror test," McKay was almost certainly referring to a well-known poem that seemed especially popular in professional football circles. For example, Bill Parcells recited it when retiring from his illustrious career as an NFL head coach, and has been erroneously credited on occasion as the poet.

The Guy in the Glass, about the importance of living a life of integrity, was written in 1934 by Peter "Dale" Wimbrow, Sr. He died in 1954, but his children still faithfully preserve and protect the gift he left for us.

You can read the entire poem at http://www.theguyintheglass.com/gig.htm.

It ends with these powerful words:

You can fool the whole world down the pathway of years,
And get pats on the back as you pass,
But your final reward will be heartaches and tears
If you've cheated the guy in the glass.

So, if you're the guy—or the gal—who can look in the mirror and see a friend, someone you're proud of, congratulations on being a person of integrity.

Earlier, I mentioned sportswriter Grantland Rice and his quote about how a round of golf reveals the character or the integrity of a player. What's probably Rice's most famous quote describes the ultimate measure of one's integrity, no matter what field of endeavor he or she has chosen in life.

For when the One Great Scorer comes
To mark against your name,
He writes – not that you won or lost –
But how you played the Game.

FOOD FOR THOUGHT

- Your harshest critic should be the man in the mirror. In addition, the same person should be your biggest fan.

- At the end of the day, you know what's right. Even if initially, for whatever reason, you head down the wrong path, then change course, make it right, learn and move on.

IN OTHER WORDS

Set your expectations high; find men and women whose
integrity and values you respect; get their agreement on a
course of action; and give them your ultimate trust.
~ John Akers

Let unswerving integrity ever be your watchword.
~ Bernard M. Baruch

Integrity has no need of rules.
~ Albert Camus

Nothing so completely baffles one who is full of
trick and duplicity himself, than straightforward
and simple integrity in another.
~ Charles Caleb Colton

Nothing is at last sacred but the integrity of your own mind.
Absolve you to yourself,
and you shall have the suffrage of the world.
~ Ralph Waldo Emerson

Men of integrity, by their very existence,
rekindle the belief that as a people we can live
above the level of moral squalor. We need that belief;
a cynical community is a corrupt community.
~ John W. Gardner

Whenever you do a thing,
act as if all the world were watching.
~ Thomas Jefferson

Don't worry so much about your self-esteem.
Worry more about your character. Integrity is its own reward.
~ Dr. Laura Schlessinger

*You are already of consequence in the world if you are
known as a man of strict integrity. If you can be absolutely
relied upon; if when you say a thing is so, it is so;
if when you say you will do a thing, you do it;
then you carry with you a passport to universal esteem.*
~ Grenville Kleiser

*Integrity is not a conditional word. It doesn't blow in the
wind or change with the weather. It is your inner image
of yourself, and if you look in there and see a man
who won't cheat, then you know he never will.*
~ John D. MacDonald

*Integrity is one of several paths.
It distinguishes itself from the others because it is the right
path and the only one on which you will never get lost.*
~ M.H. McKee

There is no such thing as a minor lapse of integrity.
~ Tom Peters

*If you have integrity, nothing else matters.
If you don't have integrity, nothing else matters.*
~ Alan K. Simpson

*A life lived with integrity – even if it lacks the trappings of
fame and fortune – is a shining star in whose light
others may follow in the years to come.*
~ Denis Waitley

CHAPTER

Intuition: Your Guts Don't Lie!

Intuition is always learning, and though it may
occasionally send a signal that turns out to be less than urgent,
everything it communicates to you is meaningful.
Unlike worry, it will not waste your time.

~ Gavin de Becker

In his book, *The Gift of Fear: Survival Signals that Protect Us from Violence*, Gavin de Becker—an FBI profiler, security consultant, and presidential appointee—describes, in a thorough and compelling manner, the importance of intuition as an early warning system when our safety and well-being are threatened. At first glance, the words "gift" and "fear" may seem like an odd coupling, but de Becker quickly makes his case.

In his opening chapter, he writes: "I am called an expert. I may have learned many lessons, but my basic premise in these pages is that you too are an expert at predicting violent behavior. Like every creature, you can know when you are in the presence of danger. You have the gift of a brilliant guardian that stands ready to warn you of hazards and guide you through risky situations." That brilliant guardian, that early warning system, is indeed fear.

In an article in a recent issue of *Reader's Digest* (February 2013), author Kathryn Wallace affirms de Becker's findings. "Fear," she writes, "should be our best friend. It's a chemical reaction, a signal to pay attention to a threat. It's our brain alerting us to danger, triggering the classic fight-or-flight response . . . to help us survive."

Ignoring these early warnings, or red flags, can have serious consequences. When questioned about his findings during a televised interview, de Becker said: "I ask people who have been assaulted if they had any warning beforehand. Many say they couldn't put their finger on it, but they knew something was wrong. When asked, 'Why didn't you call for help?' they say they couldn't see any evidence to justify their alarm so they dismissed it. They listened to their intellect, not their instincts." In other words, they blew past those red flags.

In Times Like These

I realize I'm stating the obvious when I point out that we're living in perilous times. It seems that lurking around every corner is a swindler looking to separate you from your money, a con artist who wants to steal your company, a computer hacker looking to steal your identity, and/or some crazed young man armed to the teeth and looking to separate you from your life. The red flags are everywhere.

For example, the proliferation of websites where you're promised a match with the man or woman of your dreams has made the "dating game" about as safe to play as Russian Roulette. It's gotten so bad that it gave birth to an organization named Heartless Bitches International, which has published a detailed list of warnings that women (and, in some cases, men) should heed in developing relationships.

The last time I checked, its website listed 170 red flags (sample: #87 – He seems like "a challenge," or "a diamond in the rough."). That reminded me of this bit of advice from Mae West, a famous early twentieth century quick-witted actress and sex symbol. "Don't marry a man to reform him," she said. "That's what reform schools are for."

The new version of that quote can be found on a September 24, 2011 *Saturday Night Live* skit with Kristen Wig, who's wearing the new Chanel "Red Flag" perfume to warn men that she's "F%$#ing Crazy!"

The popularity and ubiquity of the Internet have made it easy for anyone to post red flag warnings on nearly any conceivable topic. Google the words "red flags," and you'll find more than fifty million sites. While the red flags in the relationships category are numerous, you'll find some in whatever activity you choose. Whether you're buying a car, banking online, making investments, paying bills, using Facebook, Pinterest, or any other social media, listing items on eBay or Craig's list, and on and on and on, you'll find red flags galore.

Call it what you will—intuition, instinct, a gut feeling, a hunch, a sixth sense, a red flag—fear—as de Becker (quoted above) reminds us, "it will not waste your time." The message it sends can be either negative or positive and, in either case, we'd do well to pay attention as, according to de Becker, "it always has your best interest at heart."

On the Job

If your work responsibilities involve interviewing and hiring new employees, then recognizing the wide array of red flags you're likely to encounter will make your job a whole lot easier. For example, let me tell you about a recent experience I had with a candidate for a leadership position in my organization.

This woman came with high marks from colleagues and friends. I was really looking forward to meeting her, as we needed what I was told was in her "wheelhouse" (a/k/a skill set).

Prior to any interview, I try to read from the bottom up and between the lines of the résumé, looking for gaps in work history, lateral or backward moves, verbiage which sounds extreme or over the top. For example, one candidate wrote: "Using Six Sigma techniques and tools, I took the company from losing $1 million a year to making more than $4 million per year." Really? This was on the résumé of someone applying for a middle manager role who had completed the complex and detailed Six Sigma certification process just one year earlier.

Getting back to my prospective hire, I saw no gaps in her history. I knew from talking to others that she had started a business which was failing. From my read of the situation, the business was a bit ahead of its time and would be difficult to scale, even in the best circumstances. Nevertheless, the fact that she had picked herself back up and was out trying again is a huge positive, provided the person learns a few things.

We scheduled a meeting at my very utilitarian, low rent office. Real estate people would call it a "Class C." My office is basically in a loft above a hangar which houses two planes and a helicopter, partially visible through a couple of windows on one side. The entire office is adorned with airplane memorabilia, photos, prints, propellers, you name it. If it's aviation related, it can be found in my office.

I heard her come in the front door and she was greeted by some teammates on the first floor. She walked up the open staircase and turned and looked at me. The second our eyes met, something in my gut yelled "Red Flag!" I'm not sure why; something just wasn't right. She was well dressed, attractive, and seemed very poised; yet there was just something about her that had triggered that sixth sense.

After practicing medicine for more than twenty-seven years, I've gotten fairly good at trusting my gut, at least as far as patients go. There are times when I've treated patients and can't figure out precisely what's wrong. I just know something is seriously wrong with them and that someone needs to figure it out. More often than not, I'm right. This trait isn't special to me; all my emergency medicine colleagues have some degree of "gut instinct," which probably grows with the number of grey hairs.

The prospective executive sat down and began to talk. One thing about my interview style is that I like to ask questions designed to learn about the person, not simply the role. I leave it to my teammates to ask the detailed knowledge-based questions. I ask what I consider are the simple but hard questions, designed to see if the applicant will fit in our environment, work well with our team, persevere during adversity, be kind, compassionate, and trustworthy.

She told me her business was on the block to be sold and that she was entertaining multiple offers to purchase it. I thought this was rather odd, because just a moment earlier she told me she was "winding down her business." I asked her a few questions about the incongruity between "winding down" and "entertaining multiple offers." She danced around the answers for a bit before blurting out, "Did you used to fly?" Now, I know I'm nearly as old as Moses, but I'm still kicking and as long as I can pass my flight physical and am still breathing, I will be flying. I responded, "Actually, I still fly."

She then went on to tell me she'd done some consulting work out at Luke Air Force Base on one of their health care initiatives. As a reward, she said they "gave me a ride in an M-35." Somewhat incredulous, I asked: "Do you mean an F-35?" She said, "Yeah, you know, the new one. It made me kind of sick to my stomach but it was really fun!"

Directly in her line of sight is a framed 24"x 36" picture of me and an F-16 Squadron Commander, call sign "Wyatt," on the wall, standing in front of his plane. We're both dressed in flight suits and still stuffed into our "G" suits. One of us looks a bit worse for the wear but is wearing an ear-to-ear smile—me. From 2010 to 2012, I was an honorary commander at Luke and had the great fortune to fly with Wyatt in his F-16.

At this point in our interview, she was "Tango Uniform," a military slang term roughly meaning "broken beyond repair; dead." First, there are no two-seat F-35s. Second, no F-35 had yet landed at Luke. Third, to quote the Base Commander, "No civilian, except celebrities and honorary commanders, gets rides in an F-16 and no one gets a ride in an F-35."

I didn't call her on it. There was no point. I wasn't going to hire her, no matter what else she said. Anyone who lies to my face about an area where I have at least some rudimentary knowledge is pathological.

I knew none of this before she first arrived in my office. Yet, for some reason, my internal alarm system had been triggered the moment I first saw her.

Proceed with Caution

Over the years, I've kept a list of things that should make the hair on the back of your neck stand up. The following is a sampling of the red flags I've collected. Some are specific to the medical profession, but others may be helpful for anyone charged with screening prospective employees.

- Don't hire anyone who's rude to your receptionist or assistant.

- Arrogant people rarely improve their demeanor.

- Laziness and negativity are contagious; eradicate the source or it will infect your entire staff.

- Flirting during an interview is always a red flag.

- Before interviewing prospective employees, check their MySpace and Facebook pages. Comments like, "Thanks for the great weed, dude," should be worrisome.

- Snapping gum, chewing with mouth open, saying "Like" and "Ya know" every sentence are not positive signs.

- The tougher the pre-hire negotiation, the higher maintenance the employee.

- Applicants who "hit on your staff" during their interview process are never good hires.

- With employees who insist they're doing their best when obviously they're well below the mark, believe them—and then free them to find work elsewhere.

- You can't teach kindness or compassion; if a caregiver doesn't demonstrate those characteristics, he or she should be working in a solo job.

- "My prescription for Percocet fell in the toilet; was eaten by my dog; was stolen; etc." is a red flag, especially in the medical field.

- When nurses say, "Are you sure you want to discharge this patient?" rethink your options.

- Providers who were accused/convicted of having sex with patients are probably not "good hires."

- Never hire someone who, in the job interview, identifies "turning my boss in to OSHA" as his greatest contribution at his last job.

- Employees who call in sick three days before their shift should raise suspicion.

- Think carefully about hiring candidates whose fingernails are stained with nicotine and whose clothes or hair smell like smoke; their smoking breaks will outnumber their productive work hours.

- Candidates with tattoos of swastikas or other hate groups, or of "Mom" spelled incorrectly, bear special consideration.

Parenthetically, that last one reminded me of a brief item that appeared in a leading sports magazine some years ago. It seems that a certain well-intentioned football player at a well-known university had his mother's first name, which is MABEL, tattooed in four-inch-high letters on his chest. The problem: he spelled it MABLE! Definitely a red flag.

Feel free to use any of these red flags as your own. They've certainly saved me a few times when I might otherwise have gotten into trouble. Some may even keep you out of court or help you avoid some problems in your business or professional activities.

A "Eureka" Moment

As important a role as intuition serves to warn us of impending danger, it serves an equally important one in motivating and inspiring us to set forth on paths we may never have previously considered. For example, I recently learned the story of a Southern California-based speaker, consultant, and author named Greg Godek. Greg's business background was in advertising, and for ten years he also taught an adult education class on romance.

One day his sixth sense, his intuition—that still small voice—or however you choose to describe it, whispered to him: "Greg, you ought to write a book about romance." At that moment, recognizing how much he'd learned during those ten years, he decided to "listen to my heart." It was 1991, and up to that point he'd never even thought about writing a book. But with that decision made, there'd be no stopping him. "After teaching about romance for all those years," he said, "I knew the topic inside out. So the writing process was a one-month, 16-hour-a-day brain dump."

But that was only step one. Once Greg got started, he was determined to keep moving. "My favorite quotation," he says, "is from David Lloyd George: 'Don't be afraid to take a big step if one is indicated. You can't cross a chasm in two small jumps.'" So when he learned that a traditional publisher would take from 12 to 18 months to bring out a new book, he immediately took that big step and decided to self-publish.

In order to pursue his dream, Greg quit his job, designed and printed his book, which he titled *1001 Ways to Be Romantic*, and showed up at Book Expo America, the annual industry trade show. "I was green and wide-eyed," Greg recalls. "But I'm a fast study. I learned that publishing isn't brain surgery—but it is rocket science! So by working my butt off and mortgaging my house, I made it happen." Within a few months, his book was on bookstore shelves.

For other first-time authors, that might have been "mission accomplished," but Greg was just getting started. He knew instinctively that he was on to something big, so he embarked on a book-signing tour. This wasn't the typical kind spent sitting in bookstores and autographing some books. Instead, Greg bought an RV, wrapped it in graphics that looked like a romantic movie poster featuring the cover of his book, and hit the road. It became what was then—and may still be—the most extensive book signing tour in the history of publishing.

Over a period of two years, Greg traveled back and forth across America four times, visiting forty-three states. How successful was the journey with this author-publisher-marketer at the wheel every mile? Well, his book sold more than two million copies during those years. Along the way, he attracted major media interest, resulting in appearances on *Oprah* and *The Phil Donahue Show* and mention by Jay Leno in one of his monologues on *The Tonight Show*. He was also featured in major newspapers and magazines.

Greg has continued to write and credits much of his success to his fifteen-year career in advertising and to "my relentless pursuit of publicity." At the same time, he is quick to note that writing "was not my chosen profession, but the following of a muse."

In his essay titled *Self-Reliance,* the well-known 19th-century writer and poet Ralph Waldo Emerson penned this sound advice: "A man should learn to detect and watch that gleam of light which flashes across his mind from within."

That gleam of light, that flash of intuition, can serve us all well, both in moments of danger and of inspiration.

FOOD FOR THOUGHT

- From my experience, women have better gut instincts than men, but are less likely to follow them.

- If you reflect on times when you did and did not follow your gut, I think you'll come to the same conclusion as I have.

• My gut has saved me, my patients, and certainly my businesses. The rare times when I haven't followed my instincts have been nearly unrecoverable.

IN OTHER WORDS

Listen to your inner voice for it is a deep and powerful source of wisdom, beauty and truth, ever flowing through you. Learn to trust it, trust your intuition, and in good time, answers to all you seek to know will come, and the path will open before you.
~ Caroline Joy Adams

Spend time every day listening to what your muse is trying to tell you.
~ Saint Bartholomew

Trust your hunches. They're usually based on facts filed away just below the conscious level.
~ Joyce Brothers

Good instincts usually tell you what to do long before your head has figured it out.
~ Michael Burke

A hunch is creativity trying to tell you something.
~ Frank Capra

There is only one way in the world to be distinguished. Follow your instinct! Be yourself, and you'll be somebody. Be one more blind follower of the blind, and you will have the oblivion you desire.
~ Bliss Carman

Intuition comes very close to clairvoyance;
it appears to be the extraordinary perception of reality.
~ Alexis Carrel

Intuition is a sense of knowing how to act spontaneously,
without needing to know why.... Open your thoughts to the
probability that you are more intuitive than you realize.
~ Sylvia Clare

People are never more insecure than when they become
obsessed with their fears at the expense of their dreams.
~ Norman Cousins

You have to master not only the art of
listening to your head, you must also master
listening to your heart and listening to your gut.
~ Carly Fiorina

The operation of instinct is more sure
and simple than that of reason.
~ Edward Gibbon

It is always with excitement that I wake up in the morning
wondering what my intuition will toss up to me,
like gifts from the sea.
~ Jonas Salk

Intuition is a spiritual faculty and does not explain,
but simply points the way.
~ Florence Scovel Shinn

Following my muse has worked out pretty well so far.
I can't see any reason to change the formula now.
~ Chris Van Allsburg

The Rare Find: Become the One of a Kind

All people are created with the equal ability to become unequal.
Not everyone is equipped with the same talents, gifts or abilities.
Each of us is created in a unique way. Our personalities are as
diverse as the universe itself. Yet there is one constant: We can, by
using what we have to the fullest, stand out from the crowd.

~ Glenn Van Ekeren

Are you that one-in-a-million person who stands out from the crowd? Before you answer that question, consider these words by Emmy Award-winning writer and comedian A. Whitney Brown: "There are a billion people in China. It's not easy to be an individual in a crowd of more than a billion people. Think of it. More than a BILLION people. That means even if you're a one-in-a-million type of guy, there are still a thousand guys exactly like you."

Is Brown on to something here? Could there be a thousand, or even a few hundred, guys—or gals—exactly like you? Well, using China as an example is a bit of an exaggeration. In the first place, the population of the U.S. is about three hundred million. Assuming one-third of those are children and that the rest are split evenly between men and women, there are theoretically "only" about a hundred folks exactly like you.

Considering what Brown does for a living, it's probably safe to assume that his comment was primarily to generate some laughs. Perhaps, but there's an old saying that "Many a truth is often spoken in jest." Sure, there are probably lots of folks who have many of the same characteristics and talents you or I have. Nevertheless, there's no one, not even an identical twin, who's like you in every way. Don't settle for being one-in-a-million, or billion, or trillion. Even if you have, so far, been just part of the crowd, you don't have to stay there.

Peacock or Penguin?

There's a wonderful book titled *A Peacock in the Land of Penguins* that makes this point beautifully. Written by B.J. Gallagher Hateley and Warren H. Schmidt, it's the story of Perry the Peacock, who somehow finds himself in the Sea of Organizations, where the penguins are "In Charge!" Other kinds of birds may enter but are expected to change and to "fit in."

Perry felt welcomed at first but soon the grumbling began. "You're too flashy for us," he was told and was urged to put on a penguin suit and to learn to waddle, as all good penguins do. When he asked why, he was told, "This is the way we do things here. You need to conform." It didn't take Perry long to realize he was out of place in that think-alike, dress-alike, sound-alike, live-alike world.

One day, Sara the Seagull told Perry that on one of her flights she'd spotted a place called the Land of Opportunity, where different perspectives were not only permitted but were encouraged. That was all Perry needed to hear and he quickly left the Sea of Organizations behind. He was warmly welcomed in the Land of Opportunity and quickly learned that it was much more than a place—it was a state of mind, where new ideas were eagerly accepted. Perry, resplendent in his bright feathers, knew he had found a home.

This isn't meant to say that conformity is always bad. Sometimes we have to "go along to get along." Hopefully those times are rare and knowing when to stand out and when to fade in is an integral skill set to learn.

The Sea of Sameness

Debbie Allen is a very successful entrepreneur, marketing consultant and much-in-demand professional speaker. She's also the award-winning author of the best-selling book, Confessions of Shameless Self-Promoters. Debbie wouldn't last very long in the Land of Penguins. For example, she's not one to shy away from opportunities to promote her products and services—quite the opposite. In the opening chapter of her book she writes: ""If you aren't willing to promote your talents, expertise and products, others will quickly pass you by. The world is not going to beat a path to your door unless you pave the way."

One of Debbie's favorite sayings is: "If you don't toot your own horn, you can't enjoy the music." At the same time, she fully recognizes the need to back promotion with performance. Otherwise, you'll be quickly dismissed as a blowhard. That's true for entrepreneurs, professionals, business leaders, and all those who aspire to succeed in whatever field they choose.

Keep on the lookout for the warning signs of "forced conformity." They go something like this:

- We tried it once and it didn't work.
- We've never done it that way.
- It's never been tried before.
- We've always done it this way.
- Don't rock the boat.
- If it ain't broke, don't fix it!

Of course, those aren't reasons, but excuses—excuses to keep from sticking your neck out, to dare to be different, to challenge the status quo. How much better to follow Debbie Allen's advice, "To be successful, you can't keep swimming in the sea of sameness."

If It Ain't Broke . . .

Unless you're in at least your late 40s, the name Bert Lance may mean nothing to you. He first came to prominence in early 1977, when newly elected President Jimmy Carter appointed him Director of the Office of Management and the Budget (OMB). A banker and fellow Georgian, Lance perhaps received the appointment as a reward for his service to Carter during the 1976 presidential campaign.

Lance's tenure at the OMB ended within a few months. He resigned as a result of certain charges leveled at him for actions which took place prior to his appointment, charges for which he would later be acquitted and which have no bearing on this story.

What Lance is probably best remembered for was a comment he made during an interview with *Nation's Business*, a publication of the U.S. Chamber of Commerce. Lance told his interviewer he had a solution to the federal government's spending excesses. "If it ain't broke, don't fix it," he said, adding, "That's the trouble with government: fixing things that aren't broken and not fixing things that are broken."

He wasn't the first to use the "ain't broke" statement, a bit of long-held Southern-style wisdom. But it did give Bert Lance his moment in the spotlight, and the term, unfortunately, quickly became the mantra of the status quo crowd, along with such bromides as "Don't make waves," and the others listed above.

Lance's "ain't broke" statement isn't only bad grammar—it's bad advice. It's the battle cry of the bureaucrat, the slogan of the status-quo slaves, and the mantra of the risk averse. There's always going to be a better way, a smarter way, an easier way, a faster way, a different way, a more useful way, a more creative way, and a more profitable way.

If it ain't broke, go ahead and break it and come up with a better way to put it back together. Don't just accept things as they are. Ask questions: Why is it that way? How can we improve it? What other applications can we find for it?

Follow the advice of contemporary artist Jasper Johns: "Take an object. Do something to it. Do something else to it." Figure out how you can fix it, change it, and improve it. You might be surprised at how creative you can be.

Consider this advice from one of America's greatest inventors, Alexander Graham Bell: "Don't keep forever on the public road. Leave the beaten path occasionally and dive into the woods. You will be certain to find something that you have never seen before. One discovery will lead to another and before you know it you will have something worth thinking about to occupy your mind. All really big discoveries are the results of thoughts."

Choosing the Right Path

Among my favorite poets is Sam Walter Foss, born in New Hampshire in the mid-nineteenth century. His best-known poem is probably The House by the Side of the Road, but one of my favorites is titled The Calf-Path. It's a bit too long for this space but it tells a great story. Here are the opening lines:

One day through the primeval wood
A calf walked home as good calves should;
But made a trail all bent askew,
A crooked trail as all calves do.
Since then three hundred years have fled,
And I infer the calf is dead.
But still he left behind his trail,
And thereby hangs my moral tale.

As the years passed, other animals began following that same path: First came the dogs, then a sheep, then flocks of sheep, and finally horses and men. In time, the well-worn crooked path became a lane, and then a village road, a city street, and a thoroughfare across a continent. Foss continues:

A hundred thousand men were led
By one calf near three centuries dead. . . .
For thus such reverence is lent
To well-established precedent.

A moral lesson this might teach
Were I ordained and called to preach;
For men are prone to go it blind
Along the calf-paths of the mind,
And work away from sun to sun
To do what other men have done.

They follow in the beaten track,
And out and in, and forth and back,
And still their devious course pursue,
To keep the path that others do. . . .

Another Foss poem I like is *The Man from the Crowd*, which paints a different picture. Here are the last of its four stanzas:

And where is the man who comes up from the throng
Who does the new deed and who sings the new song,
And makes the old world as a world that is new?
And who is the man? It is you! It is you!
And our praise is exultant and proud.
We are waiting for you there – for you are the man!
Come up from the jostle as soon as you can;
Come up from the crowd there, for you are the man –
The man who comes up from the crowd.

How do Foss's words resonate with you? Are you among those who "work away from sun to sun, to do what other men have done?" Or are you the man, or the woman, "to do the new deed and sing the new song?"

Here's what they mean to me. Don't be a follower. Learn from others, emulate the traits you find worthy, stay away from the ones that won't work for you. Whether you succeed or fail, it will be yours to revel in or learn from. There's no one better than you to determine what works best. So stand on the shoulders of giants, look beyond their horizon, chart your own course, and go for it.

Keep Pursuing

Have you noticed that action and success seem to go hand in hand? People of action are the ones who are finding success. Sitting on your backside, waiting for it to happen is no way to live life or be an entrepreneur and a leader. You have to work harder and smarter than everyone else. Everyone has the ability to do this, if he or she so chooses. But whatever you do, don't let your life pass and bemoan what could have been when you have all the tools to do it, to set the pace.

One of the most often overlooked aspects of leadership is the need for pursuit. Great leaders are never satisfied with traditional practice, static thinking, conventional wisdom, or common performance. In fact, the best leaders are simply uncomfortable with anything that embraces the status quo. Leadership is pursuit—pursuit of excellence, of elegance, of truth, of what's next, of what if, of change, of value, of results, of relationships, of service, of knowledge, and of something bigger than themselves

Here's the thing—pursuit leads to attainment. What you pursue will determine the paths you travel, the people you associate with, the character you develop, and ultimately, what you do or don't achieve. Having a mindset focused on pursuit is so critical to leadership that lacking this one quality can sentence you to mediocrity or even obsolescence. The manner, method, and motivation behind any pursuit is what sets truly great leaders apart from the masses. If you want to become a great leader, become a great pursuer.

Refusing to embrace pursuit is to surrender opportunity to others. Leaders who fail to pursue clarity find themselves looking through the fog. Their failure to pursue creativity relegates them to the routine and mundane. Their failure to pursue talent condemns them to a world of isolation. Their failure to pursue change breeds apathy. Their failure to pursue wisdom and discernment subjects them to distraction and foolishness. Their failure to pursue character leaves a question mark on their integrity. Let me put this as simply as I can—you cannot attain what you do not pursue.

Smart leaders understand it's just not enough to pursue, but pursuit must be intentional, disciplined, focused, consistent, aggressive, and unyielding. You must pursue the right things, for the right reasons, and at the right times. Perhaps most of all, the best forms of pursuit enlist others in the chase. Pursuit in its purest form is highly collaborative, very inclusive, and easily transferable. Pursuit operates at greatest strength when it leverages velocity and scale.

I also want to caution you against trivial pursuits—don't confuse pursuit with simple goal setting. Outcomes are clearly important, but as a leader, it's what happens after the outcome that you need to pursue. Seek dissenting opinion, pursue discovery, develop your ability, unlearn by embracing how much you don't know, and find the kind of vision that truly does see around corners. Don't use your pursuits to shift paradigms, pursue breaking them. Knowing what not to pursue is just as important as knowing what to pursue.

It's important to keep in mind that nothing tells the world more about leaders than what or who they pursue—that which you pursue is that which you value. If your message to your organization is that you value talent, but you don't treat people well and don't spend time developing the talent around you, then I'd suggest you value rhetoric more than talent. Put simply, you can wax eloquent all you like, but your actions will ultimately reveal what you truly value.

Lastly, the best leaders pursue being better leaders. They know that to fail in this pursuit is nothing short of a guarantee they'll be replaced. All leaders would be well served to go back to school on what I refer to as the science of *pursuitology*.

The Fifth Element

The Greeks had a word for it. They called it *pempte ousia*. To the Romans, it was *quinta essentia*. In ancient times, these names were given to a concept that attempted to explain what was otherwise unexplainable.

The Greeks, the Romans, and their counterparts in other civilizations believed everything in the world was made up of four basic elements: air, earth, fire and water. That theory seemed to work, except with humans. Man was obviously something more, something that set him apart from the rest of creation.

Therefore, the logic went, there had to be a fifth element, a *quinta essentia*, that gave man the power to think and talk, and that caused him to seek after God. Of all the species that have ever inhabited the earth, *homo sapiens* alone builds altars. No matter how primitive or how advanced the culture, man worships someone or something, driven by this innate element, this *quinta essentia*, or quintessence.

Over the centuries, the word "quintessence" has taken on broader meanings. Its definitions include: the consummate instance; the most perfect manifestation of a quality or thing; the purest form of anything; and the transcendent specimen of a given class.

In today's disposable, biodegradable, assembly-line, cookie-cutter society, the quality of quintessence, this "consummate instance," this "most perfect manifestation," this "transcendent specimen," has been lost—sacrificed on the altars of mediocrity and imitation?

Authors Betty Cornfeld and Owen Edwards beg to differ. In their wonderful book, *Quintessence: The Quality of Having It*, they claim that "Quintessence lives, as vitally as ever; it's just harder to discern amid the undistinguished plenty of our times."

Cornfeld and Edwards also note that, "With the advent of mass production, the odds against quintessence grow and have continued to grow... Since the Industrial Revolution, it has become possible to assume that quintessence is inconsistent with mass production and the premise is hard to deny."

Just as the ancient Greeks and Romans believed in the four basic elements of air, earth, fire and water, so many of today's business and professional men and women seem to focus on the four elements of volume, profits, cash flow, and net worth as the ingredients of success. Little thought seems to be given to the "fifth element," the quintessential, the quality that separates the very good from the very best.

Today, in our personal and professional lives, can we become that "perfect example," that "transcendent specimen?" Quintessence is a rare and multi-faceted jewel, "always there to be found. It is the good news, shining through the bad."

In the words of Cornfeld and Edwards: "Although quintessence cannot be found in abundance in our claptrap age, its ancient voice still whispers beneath modern exteriors and we do well to recognize it and seek it out."

The rare find! The one of a kind! Let the quest begin!

——————— FOOD FOR THOUGHT ———————

- What I look for in job applicants, and in me, is a drive to constantly become better. It could be "better" at something trivial, but it's still an improvement. The next time you conduct an interview, or even when you're talking to a friend, ask: "How are you bettering yourself?" In most people, the thought of continued improvement never crosses their mind. Now that it's crossed yours, you're well ahead in the game!

———————— **IN OTHER WORDS** ————————

There is some work that will never be done if you don't do it.
There is someone who would miss you if you were gone.
There is a place that you alone can fill.
~ Jacob Braude

Every human being is intended to have a character of his own,
to be what no others are, and to do what no other can do.
~ William Ellery Channing

Don't rely on someone else for your happiness and self-worth.
Only you can be responsible for that. If you can't love and
respect yourself—no one else will be able to make that happen.
Accept who you are—completely; the good and the bad—
and make changes as you see fit,
not because you think someone else wants you to be different.
~ Stacey Charter

By being yourself, you put something wonderful in the world
that was not there before.
~ Edwin Elliot

You're irreplaceable. Without your voice, your passion,
something is missing from the conversation.
Whatever you bring, we need it. We need you. It's true.
~ Holley Gerth

What another would have done as well as you, do not do it.
What another would have said as well as you, do not say it.
What another would have written as well, do not write it.
Be faithful to that which exists nowhere but in yourself.
~ André Gide

*The individual is the true reality of life. A cosmos in himself,
he does not exist for the State, nor for that abstraction called
'society,' or the 'nation,' which is only a collection of individuals.*
~ Emma Goldman

*The individual has always had to struggle to keep from being
overwhelmed by the tribe. If you try it, you will be
lonely often, and sometimes frightened. But no price is too high
to pay for the privilege of owning yourself.*
~ Friedrich Nietzsche

*You've gotta be original, because if you're like someone else,
what do they need you for?*
~ Bernadette Peters

*If you're not prepared to be wrong,
you're not prepared to be original.*
~ Sir Ken Robinson

*Individuality is the salt of common life.
You may have to live in a crowd,
but do not have to live like it, nor subsist on its food.*
~ Henry Van Dyke

CONCLUSION

I know—you already knew all this. What you may have once forgotten is now back in the front of your brain. "This is not rocket science," you muttered once or twice.

You're right, it isn't. Everyone knows every concept in this book. Some of us gobbled it up at the dinner table, dished up by caring parents and siblings. If you weren't fortunate enough to get it at home, you surely heard at school or from your friends or colleagues.

Now that you're reminded, share it with others. They may need to be reminded as well. It's always the simplest concepts—kindness, integrity, humility, perseverance, optimism—that are the most meaningful, or sometimes the most distressing when they're missing from someone's DNA.

ACKNOWLEDGMENTS

This book has been a work in progress for over three decades and would not have come to fruition without the help of a number of individuals to whom I am profoundly indebted.

Bob Kelly helped me organize a large number of my disparate journal articles and lecture notes into a workable manuscript. In addition, he provided a wealth of information and anecdotes laced with his own personal experience. Without Bob's ability, work ethic, and diligence, this work could not have been completed.

Vickie Mullins and **Brandi Hollister** of Perfect Bound Marketing, for their excellent work on the interior design and layout of the book.

Fabrizio Romano whose creative assiduousness shines brightly on the cover.

Finally and most importantly, to many **great friends** and **my family** who spent an untold amount of time beta-reading chapters and offering invaluable insight and suggestions.

ABOUT THE AUTHOR

John Shufeldt is a serial student, an indefatigable change agent and a multidisciplinary entrepreneur who has studied the traits and qualities of extraordinary individuals for over three decades.

John received his BA from Drake University in 1982 and his MD from the University of Health Sciences/ The Chicago Medical School in 1986. He completed his Emergency Medicine Residency at Christ Hospital and Medical Center in 1989 where he spent his final year as Chief Resident. John received his MBA in 1995, and his Juris Doctorate in 2005, both from Arizona State University. He is admitted to the State Bar in Arizona, the Federal District Court, and Supreme Court of the United States. His certifications include Fellow, American Board of Emergency Medicine, Fellow, College of Legal Medicine, and American College of Emergency Physicians.

He founded numerous health and non-health care businesses and continues to practice emergency medicine and law. He is the business manager and one of the founding partners of Empower Emergency Physicians and continues to practice emergency medicine at St. Joseph's Hospital and Medical Center. In 2010 John started MeMD, an on-demand virtual health care venture designed specifically to improve access to and reduce the cost of health care.

An avid rotor and fixed wing pilot, he holds a multi-engine Airline Transport Pilot rating and is type-rated in a North American T-28 and Citation 510. John has been actively involved in law enforcement as a "SWAT Doc" since 1998 and is currently Medical Director of the Phoenix Police SWAT team. He is Past President of the Board of the Men's Anti-violence Network, and serves on the Drake University Board of Trustees and the Sandra Day O'Conner College of Law Alumni Board.

John has authored and co-authored books on Children's Emergencies and Contract Issues for Emergency Medicine Physicians. He writes and lectures on a variety of subject matters to graduate medical, business and law students. He is the Health Law Editor and on the Advisory Board for the Journal of Urgent Care Medicine and was the Editor in Chief of *Urgent Care Alert* and *ED Legal Bulletin.*

He is an adjunct professor at the Arizona State University, W.P. Carey School of Business where he taught Health Law and Ethics to MBA and Health Sector Management students and is an adjunct professor at the Sandra Day O'Connor College of law where he teaches a seminar on Health Law Entrepreneurism.

You can find more information out about John and his work at: www.ingredientsofoutliers.com.